T0373721

THE
SPINNING
HOUSE

THE
SPINNING
HOUSE

HOW CAMBRIDGE UNIVERSITY LOCKED
UP WOMEN IN ITS PRIVATE PRISON

CAROLINE BIGGS

In memory of Daisy, Elizabeth, Emma and Jane and all the women imprisoned in the Spinning House.

Please note that the dialogue in this book is based on fact in that the historical content is taken from court records and secondary sources, but has been paraphrased to recreate the atmosphere and emotions of the events as they would have taken place.

First published 2024

The History Press
97 St George's Place, Cheltenham,
Gloucestershire, GL50 3QB
www.thehistorypress.co.uk

© Caroline Biggs, 2024

British Library Cataloguing in Publication Data.
A catalogue record for this book is available from the British Library.

ISBN 978 1 80399 570 0

Typesetting and origination by The History Press.
Printed and bound in Great Britain by TJ Books Limited, Padstow, Cornwall.

FSC
www.fsc.org

MIX
Paper | Supporting
responsible forestry
FSC® C013056

Trees for LYfe

CONTENTS

PREFACE

Cambridge University is internationally renowned for its ancient colleges. It is lauded for its educational excellence. But in the last quarter of the nineteenth century, infamy blighted its hallowed name. As an alarming number of courtroom dramas exposed the university's steadfast resolve to cling to its archaic right to lock up women in its own private prison – the Spinning House – the great institution began to look tarnished. None of those women had broken the law of the land. Yet their removal from the streets of Cambridge was deemed essential to protect the moral character of the gentlemen scholars fresh from the constraints of masters and parents.

This little-known tale of woe came to my attention after I heard the name Daisy Hopkins mentioned at a meeting of local historians. The story went that she was the girl responsible for the abolition of special laws, applicable only in Oxford* and Cambridge, permitting the arrest and imprisonment of women suspected of soliciting. Because of her, the Spinning House prison – Cambridge University's private prison for women – was torn down in 1901.

I was curious about this story. It seemed unlikely that a prostitute would be the cause of such a seismic shift. I went to the local library in search of evidence. There, I discovered that in the eighteenth century the vice chancellor had paid the town crier 10s to whip ten unruly women. How could this have happened and so few people know about it?

---

* The situation in Oxford was less brutal than in Cambridge. There, women were taken before the local magistrate and, if proven guilty, were sent to the local prison.

More research led me to a report in the *New York Times* newspaper about the trial of Daisy Hopkins. Why, I wondered, had a London barrister fought the case of a streetwalker? The titillating story didn't quite add up. In the years that followed this first discovery, my curiosity about this teenage girl niggled. Who was Daisy Hopkins? What was this prison? And did the internationally famous university really have such a murky, misogynistic past?

In 2016, I decided I couldn't leave the tale alone. A return to the archives I'd exhausted a decade before rewarded me with a document that changed everything. Someone else had been as curious as me about this untold story. And luckily, that person was like me. Her sense of injustice about what had happened to thousands of young women at the hands of a powerful group of men led her to write her Open University PhD thesis on the topic.

Every page of 'Girls of the Spinning House: A Social Study of Young Cambridge Streetwalkers, 1823–1894'* filled me with anger and outrage. Sitting in the local studies library, I paused my note-taking. All I could do was greedily devour the facts unfolding before me. Between 1823–94, senior members of the university known as proctors were responsible for over 6,000 arrests of young women. Under the common law of the land, none of those women had committed a crime. I'd uncovered a tale of overwhelming social injustice against young, working-class women.

I found, too, that Daisy Hopkins was the topic of the Law Bar Association's Annual Lecture in 1999. One of her cases against the university had made legal history. I wondered why this story hadn't broken free of academic studies. The more I discovered, the more I felt determined to change this.

Although I am Cambridge born and bred, I am not a member of the elite group of people who inhabit the 'other' side of Cambridge. I discovered I couldn't research the story until I'd gained the authority to delve into college and university archives. It wasn't enough to have a BA from the local university, as opposed to Cambridge University. I needed more before I could get inside the places where the treasure, supporting this story, lay buried.

---

* Janet Oswald, 'Girls of the Spinning House: A Social Study of Young Cambridge Streetwalkers', Open University thesis (2008).

Following a few courses in creative non-fiction writing at Cambridge University, I was offered a place at the University of East Anglia to take an MA in Biography and Creative Non-Fiction. Doors that had previously been closed to me swung open once I had a UEA email address. Now I wasn't just an amateur local historian, with a chip on my shoulder, banging on about the mistreatment of women at one the world's most famous educational establishments. I was – almost – 'one of them'; no longer a victim of the same class and gender stereotyping as the women dragged into the Spinning House. The more I read, the more furious I became about this dual reality. Women have been edited out of the history of Cambridge for too long.

I decided I wanted to write a story about the Spinning House that everyone would want to read. I wanted to discover, and reveal, as much as I could about the real lives of the young women thrown into a prison repeatedly condemned by prison inspectors. It was a damp, cold place where women would emerge in a much worse condition than when they went in.

Plenty of biographies and histories are written about the people, mainly men, who 'went to Cambridge'. Daisy Hopkins was not a member of the group of people who 'tell' or are 'told' about, in the history of Cambridge. The lives of working-class women are hard to trace. Yet, if they were summoned into a courtroom, their characters spring alive. Even then, we only know them in terms of their threat to authority. Fleshing out their back stories takes a huge amount of, often futile, research. But it is worth the effort. For then their characters come alive, and rather than seeing them as troublemakers, we see them as ordinary women searching for a way to live when paid work was hard to find and entailed long hours of drudgery.

It was over 100 years since Daisy's arrest, but for a modern-day woman, the landscape wasn't entirely unfamiliar. Rules restricting merrymaking lingered. To ensure a suitably quiet atmosphere, curbs on nightlife limited noisy activity. But those, including me, seeking Saturday night entertainment discovered we could circumvent the 'quiet' crackdown. We joined the term-time queues outside the Student Union or Graduate Centre, and sometimes we made our way to the cellars of King's College for their legendary discos.

All these venues were in the city centre, their disturbance perfectly acceptable to university authorities. And there we danced the night away, an ink splodge on one hand, a drink in the other. Mixing with townies both thrilled and scared undergraduates, a distraction their tutors still warned against. But at least they could no longer be whipped or arrested for it.

My experience of working for Cambridge University at a time when the colleges were nervously opening their ancient doors to women was that the establishment was firmly dominated by men. I worked in university libraries and always there was a moment when a 'new girl' was taken to one side by an 'old girl': 'Don't get left alone with him …' she would whisper in the junior's ear. Little had changed since the diarist and Fellow Commoner Charles Astor Bristed wrote in 1845 that many upper class men believed working women existed purely for their pleasure.

Armed with a precious reader's ticket, I booked myself a table in the Manuscripts Room of Cambridge University Library. Here, I took a deep breath as I lightly brushed my fingertips over the stiff velum pages of the three large Spinning House Committal books covering the years 1823–94. It was a thrilling moment. I glimpsed the real lives of the young women who were dragged off the streets of their hometown into a carelessly run prison.

Notes scratched in blotchy black ink in the margins revealed that some of women confessed to their 'crime', although no written confessions or statements were taken. In the vice chancellor's court, unlike a magistrates' court, no proof of wrongdoing was required. Suspicion was all – true or false. If a girl didn't 'come quietly', her sentence was lengthy. Admitting guilt of streetwalking essentially got the ordeal over as quickly as possible. But any girl finding herself inside the Spinning House, guilty or not, would be tainted by the experience, her employment prospects and those of her family plummeting. The few women who were brave or enraged enough to retaliate with legal suits provide us with fascinating facts about their real lives.

Through such court records, archive material, newspapers and other primary and secondary sources, I began to hear the voices of four girls – Daisy, Elizabeth, Emma and Jane. I heard the anguish of family members pleading for the release of a daughter or sister, and of young women recounting the hours leading up to the death of a loved friend. I heard, too, the voices of men and women up and down the country demanding an end to the cruel regime of proctorial authority. I read the justifications of an elite group of men determined to 'protect' the young men in their care by clinging to ancient laws that allowed them to control almost every aspect of the lives of the townspeople of Cambridge.

Victorian society cherished high standards of personal conduct. It gave way to an impetus for social reform, but in doing so, it also placed restrictions on the liberty of certain groups.

In Cambridge, hundreds of charming young men with time and money on their hands arrived each year – although not all were wealthy. We don't know what promises were made to the young women they flirted with, or how easy it was to win the virtue of a beguiled beauty. What we do know is that the punishment for talking to an undergraduate after dark didn't fit the crime.

ACKNOWLEDGEMENTS

I would like to thank my fellow students from the MA in Creative Non-Fiction 2018–19 cohort at the University of East Anglia who confirmed I had an important story to tell, and later the Madingley Writing group whose support was of great value. My greatest thanks for moving me from manuscript to publication must go to Nancy Lavelle Mangan, Jacqui Lofthouse of The Writing Coach and Katy Massey. I am also indebted to the staff at The History Press for their amazing editorial assistance. Final thanks go to friends and family who have accepted my reclusive habits over the past few years as I trawled archives and glued myself to my laptop. It has been a such an honour to finally tell the true story of the Spinning House.

While every effort has been made to obtain permission from all copyright holders for materials used in this book, I would welcome any new information that could provide further copyright credit in any future reprint.

INTRODUCTION

On Wednesday, 26 April 1561, Queen Elizabeth I added her regal signature to a charter sanctioning the incarceration of any woman 'suspected' of corrupting the morals of the young undergraduates at Cambridge University. It read:

> We ... grant the Vice Chancellor, Masters and Scholars and their Successors for ever, that it shall be lawful ... at all times to make scrutiny, search and inquisition ... in the town of Cambridge ... for all public women, procuresses, vagabonds and other persons suspected of evil ... whom on inquisition ... shall found guilty or suspected of evil, they may punish by imprisonment of their bodies, banishment or otherwise.*

This was the cause of centuries of bitter riot and rebellion between town and gown. The charter gave senior members of the university the right to arrest and imprison any unchaperoned woman walking in the town's streets after dark.

The inky flourish of Elizabeth's jewelled hand sealed an irksome problem. The vice chancellor pleaded for her to chastise the Mayor of Cambridge and his deputies, who had a habit of liberating the 'delinquent prisoners' the vice chancellor brought to the town jail. Back then, the women were accommodated in cells inside the crumbling town jail within the precinct of the old castle. The mayor held the keys – and the power. But an anxious vice chancellor, desperate to protect his fresh young flock of men, free for the first time from the close supervision of parents and tutors, pulled rank to demand a transfer of power.

---

* Taken from the Elizabethan Charter of 1561 – Winstanley, 1947: 92.

The young men sent to Cambridge, often second sons going 'into the church', were *in statu pupillari* – under the guardianship of the vice chancellor. It was his duty to suppress the natural urges of his young men with preaching and prayer. Newspapers and history books allude to parents' fears that precious sons, and their fortunes, might be bewitched by the cunning wiles of country girls. Or worse, they might father children they felt compelled to support. Cambridge University was ruthless in alleviating such parental terrors – all the while turning a judiciously blind eye to the gentlemen scholars 'stabling' their mistresses in the town.

The queen's decree didn't stop at allowing the round-up of suspicious women. It listed further measures. No longer would the town have rights over weights and measures, the licensing of beer, wine and theatrical performances and more. From then on, the vice chancellors of Cambridge University had power over each person and every aspect of town life. Cambridge was run for the benefit of the university, not its local inhabitants.

Little is known about the Spinning House prison, although its conditions were bad enough to lead to the deaths of some of those incarcerated there. A faded photograph of the hated building shows a squat brick and stone construction, built in the seventeenth century and originally a workhouse where the poor learnt to spin flax. The building morphed into use as a place to lock up vagabonds, petty thieves and disorderly women. During the nineteenth century, the university took control of the building.

It was said that an inhabitant of Cambridge from 1500 would have recognised the same narrow, unpaved, squalid streets and landmarks of the town in 1800. While the townspeople were concerned about their dirty and polluted yards and congested streets, the university authorities, in their open and airy courts, extended their concern to the 'debris' parading in the public streets.

In 1825, another monarch, spurred by another vice chancellor, signed another decree. An Act of Parliament was passed allowing the employment of special constables to assist the proctors in their nightly search for 'lewd' women. The 'Bulldogs', as the townspeople branded these detestable men, were employed to sniff out every idle piece of tittle-tattle about the young women living in the town. These servants of the university knew the dark alleys and troubled families living in them. They watched girls blossom into women. They whispered words into the eager ears of proctors about who to arrest, who to caution, who to turn a blind eye to.

Those women hauled into the Spinning House accused of being 'procuresses' were denied legal assistance. They stood in silence during the fifteen minutes it took the vice chancellor, resplendent in his academic garb ('academicals'), to hear the charges against them. No family or friends stood beside them.

Mistakes were made. Evidence was based on hearsay, not facts. Being in the wrong place at the wrong time could be a crime – according to laws adhered to by the university – but not according to the law of the land, where proof was needed and an appearance before the local magistrate.

As I delved deeper into the archives, I became familiar with the tragic stories of women snatched off the streets of the town they lived in. It wasn't only Daisy Hopkins who'd suffered in the cold and damp cells condemned by prison inspectors and Liberal reformers. Thousands of young women's lives had been ruined and I wanted to write about the handful of brave and enraged young women who had had the courage and determination to fight back.

1

BLOODY RIOT

It was February 1846. A Saturday – market day. It was a day when Fenland folk flocked to Cambridge to peddle goods nurtured from the famously fertile soil that bordered the town. Traders travelled far and wide to barter for such goods. But as dusk fell in the narrow streets, lanes and yards wedged against the solid walls and impenetrable gatehouses of the Cambridge colleges, unknown violence was about to bloody the pavements.

Revolution in Paris and the rising unrest of the Chartist movement breathed oxygen onto the smouldering flames of resentment festering in the dark corners of the town. Nervous that parents might be fearful of sending their sons to Cambridge if they heard that unsavoury women walked its darkened streets, the proctors had agreed to a ruthless drive of 'cleaning' the town centre of unchaperoned women. Their nerves had been rattled by the opening of a railway station on the edge of the town the previous year. Nerves were also jangling about the swelling numbers of displaced agricultural workers squeezing into the cramped streets and yards of Barnwell, a rural village now sprouting row upon row of closely packed houses. Here resided a growing number of people whose lives were independent of the shackles thrust upon most parts of the town.

Tensions between the proctors and the police had already been mounting that month. The vice chancellor objected to the way the town constables arrested and sent wayward members of the university to the local magistrate. He demanded that the mayor instruct police officers to bring members of the university before him for punishment. The mayor refused. Wasn't this exactly what the townspeople were asking to be done to the women arrested on suspicion of soliciting? They wanted the women to be judged by a magistrate, as happened in Oxford, not the vice chancellor.

Violence sparked as dusk fell, when a cluster of youths from the town rushed to free a young woman spotted in the clutches of the proctor and his men outside Trinity College. Cries of, 'Town! Town!', the well-known call to arms, rang out.

'No secret tribunals!' chanted the excited mob gathering outside Trinity. They were joined by 'pot-valiant' butchers and bargees who were in town for market day and ready for riot. Ugly skirmishes quickly escalated into one of the bloodiest riots the town had ever witnessed.

As fighting erupted between town and gown, any gownsman spotted on the streets was in deep peril. In King's Parade, a sturdy local lad named Edward Patman, whose sister had been dragged to the Spinning House for no apparent reason, hurled abuse as he raised his fists against a cap-and-gowned Thomas Hurst and his friends.

'Come on!' he baited the scholar before landing a heavy blow.

Having felled Hurst, Patman aimed for his friends' hatted heads. He laughed as they scraped in the dirt to retrieve their fallen caps. Patman, who the *Cambridge Independent* newspaper described as a 'sturdy looking fellow', received the choice of a £1 fine or one month in prison for his actions. It was not reported which he chose.

Meanwhile, as trouble worsened in other parts of the town, proctors darted onto the pavements, shepherding their flock to the safety of their colleges. One rampaging throng spotted a gowned figure – a proctor from Clare Hall ushering his scholars to safety.

'Get 'im!' yelled the angry mauderers, as the crowd rushed at him.

'Leave me to my business!' the proctor ordered as he lifted his arms to protect his soon to be hatless head. His blood bathed the pavement so close to the safety of his college.

In Bridge Street, a proctor from Magdalene College was left severely bruised and bloodied after two Swansea butchers struck him repeatedly with a sheep hook.

As word reached the vice chancellor, who feared damage to buildings would follow damage to bodies, he demanded the mayor gather up the police force to quell the unrest. Entreaties for calm from the mayor and the police restored order. But this wasn't the end of hostilities.

The following week, a shrill cry cut through the dimly lit streets. It was the rallying call for 100 gowned men seeking vengeance. They'd assembled outside Trinity College armed with pokers, staffs and any instrument that would ensure bodily harm. At the cry, they trooped towards Rose Crescent. There, they paused to take in the scene before them. A line of policemen had gathered; behind them, a jeering mob. Three yards of dung-coated dirt divided townsmen fighting for justice for the townswomen and gownsmen fighting to save their honour in the narrow lane connecting Trinity Street with the Market Square.

'Go home to your colleges,' came the order from a police constable.

Arthur Walsh of Trinity College, a Fellow Commoner, a man who, in paying twice as much as other students, was entitled to sit on the high table and in the best seats in his college chapel, shouted to his man servant, 'Go fetch my bat!' It was clear the situation was about to turn ugly.

'Down with the Peelers!' chanted the gownsmen.

'Protect the police!' countered the townsmen.

The name calling stuttered as the two sides ran out of new taunts. It was the moment for raw hatred.

The scholars linked arms, forming a tight human chain. The swell of ragged boys and brawny men ripe for riot pushed forward. The police had no choice but to defend themselves as a battery of weaponry and yells merged.

'Take that! And that!' the cries went up.

Sticks, pokers, fists and a cricket bat were wielded and injuries mounted. Surgeons rushed to the scene to bandage and stretcher off the injured. Police Constable John Freestone was forced to protect himself from Walsh's bat. Grabbing a discarded staff, he brought it down heavily on Walsh's shoulder, knocking him to the ground. As Walsh recovered and made to fight back, a second blow cracked down on his head, rendering him unconscious.

The next day, Walsh, the son of a baronet, wanted revenge for the impertinence of the attack. Despite him joining the fray armed with youthful pride and useful weaponry, he didn't take kindly to a policeman getting the better of him. A few months later, Constable John Freestone was in court charged with assault. The cold facts of the matter, as reported in the *Cambridge Independent*, made it clear that Freestone had resorted to self-defence as the violence descended into chaos. Freestone would face two weeks in prison for fighting for his life and lose his job – the price of defending himself against a baronet's son.

The town boys usually triumphed in a fight, but not that evening. Complete revenge came when the vice chancellor demanded that magistrates impose stringent measures on anyone resorting to riot. This was bad news for a man named Wilson, who couldn't read. He set about freeing a young woman from the clutches of a proctor the following week. A large crowd gathered to enjoy the spectacle. As things turned nasty, the proctor sought refuge in the Bird Bolt Inn in St Andrew's Street. Windows and lamps inside the inn were smashed as Wilson vented his anger, although the proctor remained unharmed. Wilson received a fine of £5 but was unable to pay and so was sent to labour on the treadmill for two months.

Riot wasn't working as a way of ridding the town of the proctor's patrols and the detested Spinning House.

But this wasn't the end of hostilities between town and gown. Behind the angry fists were gathering an army of men eager to flex their legal muscles against their adversary. And the following November, Michaelmas term, the untimely death of a teenage girl played into the hands of this group of educated townsmen eager to test the law of the land against the tyrannical law of the university.

2

THE UNTIMELY DEATH
OF ELIZABETH HOWE

Elizabeth (Betsy) Howe

Age: 19
Arrested: 6 November 1846
Arresting proctor: The Reverend Mr William Towler Kingsley
Charge: Suspected of being a loose and disorderly person
Sentence: Admonished and sent home with a promise to return to Fulbourn

On a cool November morning in 1846, with the sweet smell of peat in her nostrils, 19-year-old Elizabeth Howe waved farewell to her mother, father, two sisters and the souls of 10-year-old Eliza, 10-month-old Harriet and, at 22 weeks, baby Susan, who lay under the rich fenland soil of the graveyards of St Vigor's Church and All Saints Church in the village of Fulbourn, 4 miles south-east of Cambridge.

The real lives and struggles of many of the women flung inside the Spinning House remain unknown, but when searching the newspaper archives for clues about the life and death of Elizabeth Howe, the sixth of eight Howe daughters, her name appeared in column after column of closely set jet-black ink. Details of her life covered the pages of official documents. Snippets of news about the brown-haired teenage girl, who found herself in the wrong place at the wrong time, had been devoured by eager readers up and down the country.

Elizabeth had spent the summer at home with her parents, harvesting the ripe fruits that would nourish the family when winter set in. Now, as she strode across the ancient byways towards Cambridge, her face and hands still sun-kissed from outdoor labour, she hoped to gain respectable work, despite such opportunities being in short supply.

Many young women migrated to Cambridge in search of unskilled work as servants, shop girls and laundresses, or were apprenticed as dressmakers and milliners. All entailed long repetitive hours of drudgery at the mercy of their mistresses' moods. Some girls took jobs in the lodging houses accommodating undergraduates, where a chance encounter might lead to a broken promise and a ruined reputation. Others worked as chambermaids or barmaids in the many public houses and inns in Cambridge, where they might be encouraged to behave pertly towards their customers and suffer the consequences. Already, many young women whispered about emigrating, not to Cambridge, but to the other side of the world. Indeed, five domestic servants from Fulbourn soon sailed to Australia – a land offering a brighter future.

An hour after saying farewell to her family, Elizabeth arrived in Union Row, Barnwell, a place once known as the Garden of Eden where the monks of Barnwell Abbey had tended their crops. But from 1830 onwards, its green fields disappeared as developers, hungry to profit from the great influx of workers desperate for accommodation, built hundreds of poor-quality, uniform houses. The newly named streets and roads, and those who lived there, were feared by the university as their cramped conditions quickly gained a reputation for villainy – and a place where single young women in search of rent money lodged.

It was here that the newly arrived Elizabeth was welcomed by Mary Anne Rose, the landlady of 7 Union Row, a house accommodating several young women. It was 5 November, and a rowdy night lay ahead for the townspeople as undergraduates remembered the exploits of Guy Fawkes.

Removing her muddy boots, Elizabeth and Rose agreed it was best not to venture far beyond the front door that evening. So, it was four o'clock the following afternoon when Elizabeth announced she was off to meet her friend, Harriet King. The pair hadn't seen each other since Elizabeth's return to Fulbourn. They had much to talk about.

Happily reunited, the friends strolled arm in arm through the town centre where they perhaps stole a glimpse of the new winter fashions in millinery, ribbon and fabrics so recently purchased by Mrs Asplen's at No. 8 The Crescent, and Mrs Swan in King's Parade. The *Cambridge Independent* had printed an article from the *London and Paris Ladies Magazine of Fashion* – black velvet bonnets were to be worn for the promenade and plaids in every dimension were in favour for dresses.

Elizabeth and Harriet could only gaze at such delights, but it was fun to dream. And in dreaming, the girls lost track of time despite daylight having long faded. As the church bells began striking eight o'clock, Elizabeth sensed they were being followed. The girls instinctively tightened their shawls, preparing to flee.

Seconds later, plans of escape vanished. A voice boomed from behind. 'What do we have here?'

Turning around, the pair came face to face with two warmly buttoned-up Bulldogs and a proctor, the Reverend Mr William Towler Kingsley, his long, dark cloak making plain his importance.

'We know 'em,' the Bulldogs confidently informed Kingsley.

Indeed, they did know the girls. Harriet King, a particularly tall girl, had 'emigrated' to Cambridge from the village of Girton. She was always under the watchful eye of the Bulldogs.

Elizabeth, too, had been warned twice, two years ago, to keep off the streets of Cambridge and get herself back home to Fulbourn. She had disobeyed them, paying the price with a seven-day sentence inside the Spinning House in May 1846, after which she dutifully returned home as ordered.

Now, the timing was bad. The fearful friends were trapped by the proctor and his men in a street housing a reputed brothel at one end and Christ's College at the other. Their guilt was undeniable to the men about to rob the girls of their freedom.

'Bring them in,' Kingsley instructed his men.

'Excuse me,' Harriet protested, as she struggled to free herself. 'You can't take us. We've done nothing wrong. We aren't with anyone,' she pleaded, as she felt the cold brass buttons of the Bulldogs' coats dig into her body as she struggled.

Both girls knew they risked being marched off to the Spinning House if found in the company of a member of the university after dark, but, as Harriet kept saying, that wasn't the case. Elizabeth remained still, knowing resistance was punished with a harsher sentence and admitting guilt lightened the cold hearts of the men surrounding her, vindicating the necessity for their harsh treatment.

'Get on with it,' Kingsley commanded again.

The proctors were extra vigilant in clearing the streets of temptation during Michaelmas term, the first of the three terms of the academic year – this one covering October to December. The arrival of 100 or so freshmen necessitated the increased protection.

A university made up entirely of men – an elite group united by gender, class and age – needed protection, it seemed. Parents soon dashed off letters to prominent newspapers if they suspected leniency or heard reports of working-class women walking the streets at night. Support for proctorial authority came from well-to-do and nervous parents all over the county.

The ignominy of being marched along the street to the Spinning House in the clutches of the proctor and his men was mortifying and ruinous – guilt by association. Elizabeth and Harriet could do nothing but fix their eyes straight ahead during the fifteen minutes it took to reach the large oak doors of the dreaded Spinning House. The Reverend Kingsley delivered a loud knock, rousing Mr Edward Wilson, the keeper, and Eliza Pattern, his servant. The girls' names were written in the Committal Book, the charge against them inked in, 'suspected of being a loose and disorderly person'.

That night, nine of the ten cells inside the Spinning House were full, with some already being shared.

'You'll need to share,' an irritated Wilson ordered them. 'It's full.'

The trio had had a successful evening. Since the violence earlier that year, fewer men braved punishment for rescuing women in the clutches of the proctor and his men.

The girls were taken to a single unheated cell containing a night commode, candle and an iron bed with two blankets. No warm fire took the edge off the creeping fingers of dampness penetrating the entire building. They huddled together, searching for warmth as they lay on top of a damp mattress, beneath two damp blankets. Realising the relentless draught came from a small open window set just above them in an iron casing, the girls shoved the bed under the window and using the candle to shed some light on the problem, fumbled to pull at the window catch.

'It's broken,' Harriet said. 'It won't move.'

Elizabeth tried too, her fingers pulling and pushing at the cold metal bar, which was refusing to budge even a fraction of an inch. However cold they were, and however damp the bedding shrouding their shivering bodies, there was little point calling for Wilson, the keeper. He was a busy man and deaf to the tiresome pleas of inmates. The girls could only pray that when the vice chancellor arrived the next day to hear their cases, they would be sent home. After all, they hadn't been found in the company of any university men. Surely, he wouldn't imprison them for weeks on end. They had no idea what to expect.

Daybreak finally filtered through the broken window.

'Come on.' Wilson prodded a finger at them after his servant had served the girls an unappetising breakfast of weak tea and stale bread. It was eleven o'clock. 'The vice chancellor's here.'

He led them back to the small, whitewashed room they had been taken to the previous night. There sat the great man with the arresting proctor, Mr Towler Kingsley, both dressed in academic gowns.

'We found them in Hobson Street, close to a house. I suspected them of incontinent behaviour,' the proctor explained, almost by rote.

The girls remained still and silent, except when Elizabeth raised her handkerchief to stifle a cough. Neither were permitted, nor expected, legal assistance. The fact that the young women were found close to a house of ill repute and a college was enough to condemn them.

'Did they come quietly?' asked the vice chancellor.

Kingsley replied, 'Elizabeth Howe came very quietly; Harriet King did not.'

This was all the evidence produced or required. Both had been apprehended before. The vice chancellor turned to Harriet King, 'You are to stay here for two weeks.'

Her troublesome behaviour had not paid off. She knew to accept her sentence meekly, but inside she fought hard to suppress her hot fury. They had done nothing wrong according to the charter, or the law of the land, but it wasn't worth objecting.

The vice chancellor turned to Elizabeth Howe. Her throat tightened, a dizziness washed over her, she battled to stay standing.

'You may go and promise to return to your parents' house.'

Relief flooded through her entire aching body, 'Thank you, sir.'

The story of Elizabeth Howe makes for fascinating reading. I read it, pencil in hand, sitting at a desk in the Reading Room of Cambridgeshire Archives. The spine of the leather-bound book before me released a musty smell. Few had parted the creaking, parched pages contained inside. An icy thrill washed over me as I began to read. I didn't pause to make notes. I became totally engrossed.

It was almost twelve noon on Saturday, 7 November, when an exhausted, coughing Elizabeth returned to her lodgings in Union Row.

Every single step of the half-mile journey from the Spinning House inflamed her aching limbs. She clutched at her chest several times as she made the slow walk home, willing more air into her constricted lungs.

Rose was shocked at the sight of the pale and wheezing figure returning to her house. Elizabeth complained she felt 'ill all over'. Rose lit a fire for the ailing girl, but heat worsened the symptoms. There was no improvement the following day, nor the next. This was no ordinary chill. Rose was becoming anxious. A doctor would cost her dear.

'You must write to ask your mother to come,' she urged Elizabeth. 'Ask her to come quickly.'

Each day, Elizabeth's symptoms grew worse, not better, and each day, Rose expected the arrival of Elizabeth's mother. But Mrs Howe was illiterate. Unaware of the urgency, she didn't trouble to find someone who could reveal the contents of the letter.

Increasingly alarmed at Elizabeth's decline and unsure how to proceed in the absence of her mother, Rose finally called the doctor. Elizabeth had now been ill for eleven days, during which Rose had been agonising over how the doctor's fees would be paid.

Mr Charles Newby, a local surgeon, arrived to find the patient in a dreadful condition. By then, Elizabeth couldn't move her legs and arms without it causing her excruciating pain.

Examining her tongue, he found it 'much coated'. Her pulse was recorded as 120 a minute. She was extremely thirsty, yet her urine was 'scant' and 'highly coloured'.

'How did you catch such a violent cold?' he asked.

'I was put to a damp bed in the Spinning House.' Her voice confirmed her weakened state. 'The cell was cold and draughty. The window stuck open.'

Mr Newby was gravely concerned, both by her story and her condition. He decided she needed daily monitoring. Some days, he even visited twice. First, he tried a strong purgative and saline diaphoretics, but those failed to ease her symptoms. The next day, he asked Rose to make up a foot bath containing hot water mixed with a quarter of a pound of mustard and a pint of vinegar. Meanwhile, he had also been drawing urine as he believed its retention was causing problems.

'Is my mother here?' she whispered each day as she felt the strength in her body ebb away.

The days went by and nothing soothed Elizabeth's condition. A second week began, the fourth week since her incarceration in the Spinning House. Elizabeth was no longer certain if the sounds of cartwheels beyond her room were the night-soil men collecting the 'black cargo' or the milkman delivering fresh milk.

Her friends called daily to help Rose. They fetched fresh water from the nearby pump to help with the extra burden of laundry. On Monday, 30 November, she slipped into delirium.

When her friend Emma Osbourne visited that evening, a distraught Rose took her to one side.

'I'm very worried,' Rose confided. 'Fetch Newby. Ask him to bring more medicine?'

Emma hurried off into the dark streets wanting to do anything she could to help her friend. But as she neared the doctor's house, a suspicious proctor spotted her.

'What are you doing? Where are you going at this hour?' he demanded to know.

'My friend, she is seriously ill, sir. I am sent to fetch Mr Newby,' she gasped out her explanation.

'I don't believe you,' the proctor said.

'But please, I need to find him urgently,' Emma pleaded.

'Get home now or I will take you to the Spinning House.'

Fearing arrest if she refused, Emma had no choice but to return to Rose empty-handed.

At half-past one on the morning of 1 December, twenty-five days after her arrest, 19-year-old Elizabeth Howe moved from delirium to death.

Back in Fulbourn, Elizabeth's desperate note summoning her mother lay opened but unread.

3

THE CORONER'S INQUEST – DAY ONE

Daylight had faded from the ill-lit streets close to Union Row as 38-year-old Charles Henry Cooper, the county coroner, made his way towards the Old English Gentleman public house in Blucher Row, Barnwell. Two days before, a sigh had escaped from deep inside Cooper as he placed his signature on the death certificate of Elizabeth Howe. Mr Newby, who'd pronounced the death, had been clear about its cause. The narrow oblong boxes running across the official document stated that the 19-year-old single woman, living in Union Row, Barnwell, had died of rheumatic fever caused by being confined in a cold and draughty cell in Hobson's Workhouse, as many still called the Spinning House. The circumstances causing the death had been predicted; prison inspectors had repeatedly condemned the ancient building as an unfit place to lock up women. Now it was Cooper's duty to preside over an inquest that greatly saddened him.

A few days before, he'd signed another death certificate, that of a tramp, befriended by some students who had plied him with so much port the man had died. What merry entertainment the young scholars had enjoyed until its fatal outcome. The shocking circumstances sharpened his determination to seek justice for the death of Elizabeth Howe.

That cold, dark night wasn't the first time Cooper had held an inquest in the large room of the Old English Gentleman. The beery surroundings of a public house were not an unusual place to hold such a solemn event. Its commodious downstairs room, at the end of a small passage, was used for important gatherings. But this was the first time the coroner had set aside two evenings and two public buildings to accomplish the task.

The second day of the hearing was fixed to be heard in the Council Chamber inside the Town Hall. A less menacing location for the senior members of the university who, Cooper was determined, would attend this important inquiry.

The stakes were high in the matter of Elizabeth Howe's demise; the circumstances muddied by blame-shifting. Prison deaths triggered a murder investigation, or at least a case to be heard for manslaughter. Although Elizabeth hadn't died in the Spinning House itself, its role in her fatal illness had been recorded. Someone, or something, was to blame.

Charles Cooper, lawyer and eminent and celebrated antiquarian, had arrived in Cambridge some twenty years earlier to study law, though not at one of its famous colleges. He came at his own expense, purely for the pleasure of delving into its ancient documents – a man sharing my own passion for uncovering truths in dusty paperwork. His father's extensive library had been his early playground, and this had laid the foundation of a lifelong passion for historical and antiquarian knowledge.

He was admired and despised by scholars for his intelligence and was respected by all for his scrupulous judicial candour. His earliest work, *A New Guide to the University and Town of Cambridge*, published in 1831, noted, 'much of the history of Cambridge relates to the fierce and frequent disputes between Scholars and Townsmen'. He viewed Cambridge from the standpoint of an outsider and was shocked at the contrast between the two tribes inhabiting the town. One outranking the other in every way, but each grudgingly accepting the reliance they had on each other.

Cooper learnt that an inhabitant of Cambridge from the sixteenth century would still easily recognise the salient streets and landmarks of the town, despite the population having risen tenfold during that time. Overcrowding, poor sanitation and a lack of clean water added to the tensions between town and gown. It didn't help that the university elected their own MP, making it harder for the town to gain parliamentary support for change.

Cooper's forensic passion for the legal history of Cambridge led him to research and publish *Cooper's Annals*, a set of books painstakingly detailing the history of Cambridge through centuries of documents and royal charters. The university, fearing Cooper's meddling could reveal details contesting the rights and privileges they enjoyed exercising over the town, tried to get the books banned. But he boldly predicted his *Annals* would be cited more often than any other Cambridge books of his day – he was right.

But Charles Henry Cooper wasn't just a fusty antiquarian and fastidious law man. He was also a staunch member of the Cambridge Liberal Party; a supporter of the Whig Party, who strongly supported moral reform against the traditional landowning power of the Conservative Party. It was no secret he wanted to destroy proctorial authority over the women of Cambridge and tear down every single stone holding the Spinning House together.

Those for whom the university could do no wrong – whatever they did – sniggered at his bold and 'independent' opinions on law and politics. But power didn't intimidate him. What he wanted now was retribution for the death of Elizabeth Howe.

That Thursday evening, those who had squeezed along the narrow, ground-floor passage of the Old English Gentleman into the large meeting room, with its welcoming glowing fire and steady gas lighting, knew Cooper wanted to deal the university a heavy blow. Not a blow from a rioter's fist, but one to drive legal debate.

Outside, a large crowd mingled in the cold evening air, anxious to hear any snippet of information leaking from the room. Inside, two journalists, one from the *Cambridge Chronicle*, a paper loyal to the university, the other from the *Cambridge Independent*, whose allegiance stood with the town, sat poised with their notebooks.

In the large rear yard of the public house horses pricked up their ears, sensing unease. Back inside, excited chatter gave way to an expectant hush as the rotund frame of Cooper was seen rising to his feet. He fixed the crowd with commanding eyes, draped by luxuriant eyebrows. 'Silence.' His voice stilled the room in an instant.

First, he swore in the eighteen-man jury. Only men living in houses with a rateable value exceeding £10 could be called for jury service. Large juries such as this were not uncommon, but it hadn't been easy to recruit men prepared to act in a trial that might implicate the university for negligence. It was a fact that very few businesses in the town were not, either directly or indirectly, connected with the university. It didn't do to upset such a powerful master.

The 1s payment for several hours' work hadn't been a great incentive either. Thirteen men had already refused to stand. When the names and addresses of the jury, many living in Barnwell, were published in the *Cambridge Chronicle*, its readers sneered that they would 'leave it to those conversant with Cambridge to estimate the value of any opinion given by such men upon a matter affecting the character and dignity of the University'.

Having sworn in the jury, Cooper loosened his shoulders before readying himself for the evening's work. 'I call my first witness, Mr Charles Newby.'

Newby gave a detailed account of how he'd tried to save his patient's life, using several remedies, but all to no avail.

'What is your verdict as to the cause of death?' Cooper asked.

'Elizabeth Howe died of rheumatic fever,' Newby said, explaining it was an inflammatory disease that attacked the whole body, typically taking two to four weeks to kill its victim. 'What is more,' he firmly concluded, 'the severe cold inside the Spinning House was the cause of the victim's illness.'

A wave of satisfied mutterings greeted the doctor's revelation. Cooper called, once again, for silence before summoning his second witness. 'I call Mr Edward Wilson, Keeper of the Spinning House.'

Wilson was a middle-aged, round, dwarfish sort of man with a fondness for drink and an extravagant opinion of himself. A tailor by trade, he ran a small business from the Spinning House, sometimes with the aid of its inmates. He'd fitted a brass plate advertising his additional occupation on the wall outside the prison. His £60 annual salary failed to stretch to the style of living he desired; it was an open secret he was always on the lookout for ways to make it up.

That evening in the Old English Gentleman, his apprehension of awkward questioning turned him into an over-talkative and rather irritating man. A man who might have something to hide. 'Elizabeth Howe,' he told the room, 'was committed to my custody at half-past eight on the sixth of November after being delivered by the Reverend Mr Kingsley with another girl, Harriet King.'

His nerves seemed to make him want to fill in all the gaps he could find. Unasked, he launched into an explanation of how solicitous he was when selecting and purchasing goods for the prison. 'The beds,' he boasted, 'are good flock beds, as good as any poor people could wish to lie on.'

'Were you aware that the window in the cell was broken and letting in a fatally cold draught?' Cooper wanted to know.

'I didn't know the window was broken,' Wilson claimed. 'The room was,' he said, and wanted to believe, 'well protected from the weather. I saw her on the morning of the 7th, at about eight o'clock. She did not complain to me of being ill, but she did to my servant girl.' Wilson paused for a moment. 'And she ought to be here. I want nothing but the truth, why is my girl not here?'

'I would thank you to give your evidence without a speech,' Cooper dryly retorted, fixing the annoying man with disdainful glare. 'You can have any witness you like, for the inquiry will not terminate today, and any explanation you may have to offer will be listened to.'

Cooper intended to question every single person who might be able to shed light on the ten torturous hours of Elizabeth Howe's incarceration in the Spinning House. But the coroner had barely finished speaking before Wilson leapt in with more details.

'The deceased complained to my servant, Eliza Pattern, of illness. I believe the deceased had breakfast. It was provided,' Wilson was eager to deflect blame. He produced and read from the leather-bound Committal Book he had brought with him. It was the second of two cumbersome leather-bound volumes, the printed pages waiting for the inked details of each woman arrested. Each prisoner, on her first arrest, was assigned a number; the numbering started afresh with each volume. Elizabeth Howe had been assigned No. 558.

'She's been in before. Twice. Once for a week,' Wilson cried out triumphantly. 'Streetwalking,' he informed the crowded room. 'Cautioned. Twice, got seven days in May.' His smug expression suggested Elizabeth Howe got what she deserved. 'I have nothing else to add.'

'I am going to have to remind you to only answer the questions you are asked, Mr Wilson,' chided Cooper as he raised his eyebrows, a sign his patience was being tested by this annoying little man. 'It is my job to gather evidence, not yours,' he scolded as he began to lift his arm as if to clear this man away.

But Wilson piped up again. More details – real or imagined – swarmed into his head, past his deaf ears and instantly out of his mouth. 'If it is wet, I light a fire. However,' he reflected, 'on the night of the arrest it had been dry.'

Cooper moved again to brush away this bothersome man, but more information spilled from the keeper's mouth. 'She told my servant she was "lushy". But she did not appear to be intoxicated,' he added. Wilson paused to enjoy a moment of self-congratulation at his handling of the evidence.

Seizing that same moment, following a nod from Cooper, one of the jurors, who had been intimating he wanted to speak, jumped to his feet declaring, 'The mother of the deceased wishes to give her evidence and be allowed to carry the body away.'

At last Wilson was silenced. All eyes followed the coroner as he searched the crowded, lamp-lit room for female faces. Sitting quietly was a plain, 50-year-old woman, who lifted her bonneted head on hearing her name mentioned. Tears fell from her weary eyes. Mrs Elizabeth Howe had finally made it to Barnwell.

Later, the reporter from the *Cambridge Independent* informed his readers that she was 'a very respectable looking countrywoman'.

'The body can be buried,' Cooper told Mrs Howe. 'But,' he stipulated, 'the funeral must take place in the town.'

This was a heavy blow. Mrs Howe didn't know how to act – how to make any demands, how even to breathe during the longest of moments while she plucked up the courage to speak. Then her words tumbled from her lips. 'I am the mother of nine children,' she began. 'My husband is a farm labourer. I had a letter from my daughter to say she was ill, but what day it was, I don't know. She had been at home with me all summer. She had pains in her back and head.' Tears trickled down her stricken face as she declared, 'She was well when she returned to Cambridge.'

Trying to control her grief and frustration, Mrs Howe explained to the court that she couldn't read and had to find someone to explain the contents of her daughter's note. Cooper was touched by her simple honesty. 'You can have a warrant for your daughter's burial,' he kindly informed her, 'but it must be in Cambridge.'

Gathering herself up as much as she could, Mrs Howe repeated her plea for the return of her daughter's body. 'My husband is anxious to see her before she is buried. And have her placed close to three others of our children.'

'Very well' Cooper agreed. 'I will adjourn the inquest till tomorrow evening at six o'clock when it will, no doubt, be settled. And then you can have the body.'

As those who had gathered inside and outside the Old English Gentleman disappeared into the blackness of the night, Cooper mulled over his thoughts about Wilson, the keeper, a man with much to hide, Cooper suspected. How could he catch this annoying man out, he wondered, before a plan crept into his head.

Taking the Foreman of the Jury, Mr Lionel Brandon, to one side, Cooper said, 'Take a look at the Spinning House on your way home? Find another Juror to accompany you.' A surprise visit to the Spinning House might reveal the true nature of its keeper. 'Look at the cell the deceased was kept in,' he directed Brandon, 'and look at that broken window and the condition of the bedding.'

'I heard a girl died inside that prison in the reign of the old king,' volunteered an eager Brandon.

'Indeed so.' Cooper had already examined the archives. 'Elizabeth Askin, in 1828. She is noted as dying from a state of derangement and weakness. She was given a three-month sentence for being an idle and disorderly person, suspected of incontinence. During those months she became "a living skeleton",' Cooper told Brandon. 'Although her death was recorded as expiring from a "visitation of God".'

'I fear it's not the first case of neglect in that prison,' Brandon lamented, pleased to share his knowledge, before nipping off to elicit the assistance of a fellow juryman. Having selected one, the pair sped off to the Spinning House. Meanwhile, Cooper wound his way back through the tightly packed, dimly lit streets of Barnwell towards his home near Jesus College.

With each step, thoughts and doubts swarmed into his head. What was Wilson, the keeper, hiding? He had wondered for some time if the vice chancellor's right to arrest and imprison women would stand up to modern-day scrutiny. He'd read and translated the ancient charters. He had doubts. The erudite Cooper believed that the precise meaning of some of the original Latin words were open to debate.

He mulled over the that fact that, technically, the 1824 Vagrancy Law overrode the university's justification for the search and imprisonment of women. Would the Howe family be prepared to press charges for wrongful arrest if he could prove the illegality of the arrest? The university should leave it to the police and local magistrates to deal with prostitutes. Yet the police could only arrest women if there was proof of soliciting – not because they suspected it. The proctors had the upper hand.

Elizabeth Howe had not been in the company of any university men when she was arrested. Reform was needed.

A troubling story had reached him a few years earlier. A young woman of good character visited a fellow at King's College, seeking permission to attend chapel there one Sunday evening. The fellow plied her with alcohol and seduced her. On another occasion, a student summoned to his tutor's room to be reprimanded for visiting a house of 'ill-repute' was advised to do his 'whoring' in London rather than Cambridge.

Most of the senior members of the university did not believe undergraduates should be punished for falling to youthful temptations; conversely, few desired mercy to be shown to the prostitutes infesting the town. But wasn't it the case that the morals of the men needed policing, not the women?

As he ambled along Maids Causeway, almost back home, it dawned on Cooper that he should seek statements from former inmates of the Spinning House. If, as he suspected, Wilson was not the kind jailor he'd pretended to be, it would strengthen the case against him and justification for tearing down the dreadful prison. It was an unfit place to imprison women and he was determined to be the author of its decline.

While Cooper idled home deep in thought, Lionel Brandon and his companion sprang into action to undertake their important mission – their unscheduled examination of the cell in which Elizabeth Howe had been confined. The keeper was right to be nervous.

4

THE CORONER'S INQUEST - DAY TWO

As the clocks ticked towards six o'clock, half a dozen neatly dressed young women settled themselves along the narrow edge of a wooden bench in the Council Chamber of the Town Hall. Peeping shyly around the room, their fingers plucked at invisible creases in their skirts or ridges in their gloved fingers. It was clear this wasn't a place they wanted to be. Courage was needed to expose the truth about conditions inside the Spinning House. They were there, at Charles Henry Cooper's request, to give evidence against Wilson, the Keeper of the Spinning House.

The girls noticed the principal seats inside the Council Chamber – those created and reserved for the elected members of the Borough Council – were filling with gowned men. On this occasion, academics outranked the elected town dignitaries, who were forced to swear allegiance to the university at an annual ceremony known as Black Assembly. The men, uniform in their long, black gowns, embodied a powerful adversary.

Even today, at ceremonial events, senior members of the university don these same medieval costumes to process along the streets of Cambridge to mark special university events such as graduations. They do so with the confidence of a conquering army and only those inducted into its mysteries understand the nuanced codes of slightly different hoods, sleeves and robe fastenings.

Harriet King, perched on the bench with the other girls waiting to give evidence, recognised an uncomfortable-looking William Towler Kingsley, the proctor who'd arrested her and Elizabeth. Would he be blamed for her friend's death, she wondered? It was he who'd demanded their arrest, despite her protests that they weren't doing anything wrong. Could Cooper, the coroner, really win against such resistance? He'd promised that their revelations could end the might of the proctors. Despite a fire glowing in a fireplace at one end of the room, the girls huddled into the protection of their winter shawls.

Gas lamps flickered sufficiently to illuminate the determined face of Cooper, the man who was ready to decide who was responsible for the death of Elizabeth Howe. He surveyed the room with a look of satisfaction. This was his moment. Catching the peering eyes of the girls, he offered them a calming nod before calling the room to silence. Proceedings were about to begin.

Cooper's first witness that evening was Mr Newby, the doctor who had tended the dying Elizabeth and sorrowfully certified her death. 'Can you give me your account of the last days of the deceased?' he asked, since most present had not heard the detailed account given the previous evening at the Old English Gentleman in Barnwell.

Newby gave a short account of his attempts to save the life of the dying girl.

'Can you confirm the cause of death?' Cooper wanted to know.

'The cause of death was due to the deceased being put to a damp bed and catching a severe cold in the Spinning House.'

A hint of satisfaction was detectable in Cooper's voice as he called his next witness, Mr Roland Morris Fawcett, Medical Officer of the Spinning House, and a member of the Town Council. 'Would you agree the damp could have been a cause of the girl's demise?'

The girls shared glancing nods. They knew only too well of the fight to survive in that place.

'The ventilation is not as good as could be wished, or as in more modern structures,' confessed Fawcett, his accent revealing his Scottish ancestry. 'Yet,' he was at pains to point out, 'there is nothing deleterious in the state of the air nor has any disease arisen.' Fawcett was a man always ready to endorse the jurisdiction of the gowned men comfortably settled in the council members' seats.

Cooper took comfort in Fawcett's admission that the prison was antiquated, but he wanted evidence that the keeper, left to his own devices, ran the prison to suit himself rather than those incarcerated in it. 'How is the House warmed?' he asked Fawcett, using a shortened term for the Spinning House.

The coroner was asking questions to which he already knew the answer for a reason. He wanted to see every word spoken that evening printed in newspapers up and down the country. Already, he was sketching out in his mind the words he would write in his own submission to *The Times* newspaper – he was, after all, its local correspondent.

'The Keeper takes care to secure sufficient ventilation of the cells,' replied Fawcett. 'He keeps a fire going in the day rooms ... He directs his assistant to air the bedding,' he confirmed, adding, 'Before the commencement of term the cells are properly prepared for the reception of inmates.' He explained that during the long vacation – when the undergraduates went home – the Spinning House was unoccupied.

As Fawcett returned to his seat, Cooper readied himself for his next witness, William Towler Kingsley of Sidney Sussex College.

The public questioning of a proctor in a court of law was a momentous occasion. Kingsley had no option but to attend as he had committed Elizabeth Howe into the keeper's custody.

'I recollect apprehending Elizabeth Howe,' a flint-faced Kingsley clipped, 'by referring to the book of arrests. She was not behaving disorderly or indecently, but I was advised by my Constables [the Bulldogs] to apprehend her. They said they knew her to be a prostitute.'

'Do you have any instructions as to your duties, other than the statutes of the university?' Cooper enquired. The question carried the full weight of a sneer. He already knew the answer: there were no instructions – the Bulldogs guided their masters.

'I refuse to answer,' announced Kingsley.

'You must, Sir,' Cooper pressed. 'I have a duty to perform which, as Judge of this Court, I will perform.'

'I have no other instructions,' Kingsley had to confess.

'Are you familiar with the wording of the charter,' asked Cooper, who had long believed its Latin wording was open to debate.

There was a pause as Kingsley seemed to gather his thoughts. 'I have never read the charter of Queen Elizabeth giving the university power to apprehend disorderly persons,' Kingsley confessed, 'but the deceased came so quietly I recommended her discharge to the vice chancellor.'

Harriet silently cursed the man who'd given her a two-week sentence. That fateful December night, it had been too much to ask that she meekly stay silent in the face of outrageous claims. In truth, neither she nor Elizabeth had been breaking any laws, not even those diligently enforced by the university. They had not been in the company of a member of the university.

As if reading Harriet's mind, Cooper said, 'Remind me, were the girls in the company of university men that evening?' And further pressing the point, 'Were they acting in a disorderly fashion?'

'There were no members of the university in their company when we apprehended them, nor were they drunk.' Kingsley paused for a moment, struggling to defend something that suddenly seemed indefensible. But recovering, and during his sworn duty, he firmly stated, 'I believe the university has the power to arrest prostitutes in the street, even though they may not have been misconducting themselves.'

This was the very point Cooper wished to make. The proctor wasn't certain of his duties. The charter wasn't clear either.

'More than 100 arrests have been made this month,' declared Kingsley, justifying to himself, and those believing the removal of women from the streets prevented moral corruption, that the practice played a vital role in the town.

Cooper silently reflected on the fact that none of those women received a fair trial. Therefore, it was impossible to judge their guilt.

'I am guided by my constables,' the proctor repeated. 'They know the characters of local women. The keeper is answerable for the way he treats prisoners sent to him. I was doing my duty.'

Kingsley wanted to deflect blame, but he spoke the truth. Elizabeth had been arrested on the nod of the Bulldogs. But it was the keeper's disregard for the safety of his prisoners that had hastened her death.

One of the jurors signalled to Cooper. They wished to ask a question.

'Has Mr Kingsley ever been inside one of the cells?' the juror, whose name was not recorded in newspaper reports, enquired. The insult of a senior member of the university being questioned by a tradesman would have been repugnant to Kingsley, but he had to answer.

'I am not certain I have seen the interior of the cell,' came his reply, but then he recalled seeing the cell Elizabeth was taken to a few days before her arrest. 'The window was broken,' he confirmed. 'But,' he made clear, 'it is only my duty to deliver the prisoner to the keeper. What happens afterward is not my responsibility.'

A troubled and later publicly reviled Kingsley felt compelled, days later, to write a letter to *The Times* defending his actions. He argued, again, that he was only doing his duty.

But, as Cooper knew, the horrors inside the Spinning House were not unknown to the university. For over eleven years, and under as many proctors, prison inspector Captain William Williams had described the 'disgraceful state of the Spinning House'. He reported that fevers were prevalent, there was no Sunday Service and the women had nothing to do but corrupt each other – morally, they came out worse than they went in, he argued. He claimed the dons were deaf to his protests.

'Some Proctors,' he reported, 'committed women to the Spinning House with great diligence. Others turned a blind eye or escorted the women to the Female Refuge in Barnwell.' Prayer and policing did not seem to suit the conscience of every reverend proctor!

Until that day, reports about conditions inside the Spinning House had only reached the ears of those actively promoting the morals of the young men in their care. Now, with the help of six nervous women, the truth about what happened behind the closed doors of the Spinning House was about to be revealed to the public.

He turned to face the young women, raising his luxuriant eyebrows to signal the time had arrived for their testimony to be heard. Dozens of stone-faced men gazed full into the uneasy faces of each of the girls as they drew in deep breaths.

Eliza Wright was the first to speak. Only Cooper noticed how tightly she clenched her gloved hands as she willed herself to speak before the dark sea of staring faces. 'I was locked in a cell so gloomy I couldn't see how to make the bed,' she began. 'I laid down with my clothes on.' She fixed her eyes on Cooper as she spoke, for it was easier to imagine he was the only one in room.

'I saw Elizabeth Howe the morning she came out of the Spinning House. She looked cold. She put her hands to her chest as if she were ill,' Eliza recalled. 'I visited her at her lodgings after, but she was not sensible then.'

Eliza complained about the food rations in the Spinning House. 'I had to pay four pence for a loaf of bread and two pence for butter, but the two-penny worth of butter was just the size we get for a penny out of the house.'

Eliza Cook spoke next. 'I had a bad cough and sore throats due to the cold.'

Alison Walsh also complained of the cold and damp but had endured further indignity. Prone to fits, the stress of her arrest brought on an attack, resulting in water being thrown over her. 'When I got to the Spinning House in wet clothes, the proctor told the keeper to bring me dry clothes and keep me warm. He never did either.'

Then Harriet King, arrested with Elizabeth Howe, gave her account of how the two friends had tried to shut the broken window. She too, she said, had caught a bad cold that evening.

Emma Buchan remembered the beds were very short, and how the keeper ignored her pleas for water.

Emma Osbourne also described her time inside the Spinning House. 'I suffered with the cold, causing my eye to swell so much I feared I should have lost it. The food inside the prison is bad and dear and in short supply. The keeper gets it from what shop he thinks proper. We never have tea. We can't afford it. Half the time we live on dry bread. Sometimes we can have a pint of small beer, but it usually stinks. We can buy things, but we don't usually come in with any money.'

All the girls complained of the cold and damp conditions and of leaving the prison in worse health. Their accounts were later branded by correspondents of the *Cambridge Chronicle* as the 'got up tales of Barnwell streetwalkers'. Who was to be believed, they queried, a proctor or a girl from Barnwell?

Last to give evidence was Mary Anne Rose. 'The deceased arrived at my house in early November,' she said. 'She was very well then, but when she came out of the Spinning House, she complained of being ill. She said she was bitterly cold the whole of the night in her cell. I fetched the doctor on the 17th November.'

'And how long have you known the deceased?' asked Cooper.

'She has lived with me, on and off, for two years. I've never known her ill. She was a sober, gentle girl.'

The statements revealed that Wilson was not as kind as he believed himself to be.

Cooper called the keeper's servant, Eliza Pattern.

'I am the servant of Mr Wilson,' she confirmed. 'I saw Elizabeth Howe brought to the Spinning House.'

'Was she drunk?' Cooper asked.

'She told me she was lushy,' Eliza replied. 'I believe she was drunk.'

'The proctor says she was sober,' said Cooper. 'Your master says she was sober. Now what do you believe?'

The burden of being quizzed by a man of higher rank, while finding a version of the truth that would please her master, put Eliza under increasing strain. Several times she contradicted her own evidence. Eventually, she settled on the belief that Elizabeth Howe had been sober. Cooper turned his head to one side in despair.

'You are, I am afraid, a very bad girl,' he said.

Wilson sprang to his feet. 'I never caught her in a lie in my life!' he shouted. 'I have lived in this town for fifty-five years and nothing can be brought against me. Now ask her about the beds.'

Taking her cue, Eliza said, 'We have not a damp bed in the house. I air the beds with a pan of coals when they have not been slept in for a night or two.'

Possibly fearing his servant might reveal more about his custodianship, Wilson leapt in to change the subject. 'Yesterday, Mr Campion [one of the jurors] told me he did not believe me on my oath. If I had been ten years younger ...'

Cooper cut him off. 'Well, well, never mind about that,' he chided him.

'I believe she was sober,' Wilson muttered.

Cooper dismissed the foolish pair, but their jumbled performance further proved the chaotic and unkind habits of the keeper.

The next witness to be called was the Spinning House chaplain. Cooper asked him if the keeper was kind to the inmates.

'I must declare that if ever the Keeper's needful firmness borders in the least upon harshness it is fully warranted by the extreme and outrageous violence of the prisoners themselves,' he explained. 'Some are violent in their reactions to the proctor and their admission to the Spinning House. There can be swearing and loud arguments with the authorities,' the chaplain confessed.

A picture had been painted of life inside the Spinning House. It was in a parlous state and run without any care for the comforts of its inmates. If Cooper could have rubbed his hands together in glee, he would have done so.

In the cold, bright night outside, the Town Hall clocks began striking eight o'clock. Cooper asked Lionel Brandon, foreman of the jury, to report the findings of the conditions inside the Spinning House – as he had been instructed to inspect it the previous evening.

Brandon rose to his feet, and to the occasion, with pride. Steadily, he conveyed the findings of his and another jury member's unannounced visit. 'The beds were very damp with only two blankets and a rug provided. The beds were not so long as the mattress by two feet. The walls of the cells were damp, but the rooms were tolerably clean,' Brandon testified.

'And how did you find the window?' Cooper asked.

'We found the iron shutters did not fit close. A great draught is admitted which comes directly onto the head of the bed.'

With all the evidence heard, Cooper summed up. 'The jury needs to decide if Elizabeth Howe's death resulted from the cold and damp inside the Spinning House,' he stated. 'If so, whether anyone was criminally culpable.' He paused for a moment, selecting the right words. 'You might think Wilson was not so kind, yet he appears not to have known about the broken window that caused the cold. If he had, the case against him would be most serious.'

He moved to the evidence against the proctor. 'If it can be proved Mr Kingsley didn't have the power to arrest Elizabeth Howe, for she wasn't breaking the law of the land, then he faces a charge of manslaughter for violating Elizabeth Howe's liberty by forcing her into prison. She had not been conducting herself in a disorderly or indecent way at the time or been in the company of any men. But this,' he cautioned, 'will need a legal dissemination of the original charter.'

Cooper paused before delivering an unexpected speech. 'The real problem here is in the system, not the individual,' he was at great pains to point out. He knew the punishment of Kingsley or, more likely, Wilson was not what was required in the long run. 'What we need is an end to university jurisdiction. The jury cannot punish those blindly serving their master.'

For those scanning the faces of Kingsley and Wilson, they would have noticed relief loosened clenched muscles.

Cooper continued, 'The Spinning House is a notoriously improper place to imprison women.'

He was taking the stand he had planned. Planting the words that would appear in newspapers up and down the country. 'The university should send its captives to the town or county jails instead. They are run by humane men, and under the constant inspection and supervision of the magistrate who will hear both sides of the case against the accused.'

With that last rousing sentence, the jury was directed to retire. It took the eighteen men half an hour to return with a unanimous verdict.

'Do you have a verdict?' Cooper asked Brandon, the foreman of the jury.

The young women sucked in a breath. Would Wilson be found guilty of manslaughter? They prayed so.

'Yes,' Brandon paused. 'We find Elizabeth Howe died of rheumatic fever, caused by a violent cold caught at the Spinning House on the night of the 6th of November due to being confined in a cold and damp cell from the effects of which she died.'

Was this it? The moment Wilson and the Spinning House were about to tumble. But what came next stunned the girls.

'We do not find either Mr Wilson or Mr Kingsley guilty, but we have something we wish to say.'

'Say it,' Cooper urged.

'We cannot leave without expressing our abhorrence at a system which sanctions the apprehension of females when not offending against the general law of the land and confining them to a jail unfit for the worst of felons. We request that a report of the proceedings be sent to the Secretary of State for the Home Department.'

For those eager to see Wilson behind bars, especially its former inmates, the verdict came as a shock. But Cooper was delighted. The greater goal of ending university jurisdiction was in his grasp. Blaming either man was not what Cooper wanted. He wanted more. In his head, he had already written his article for *The Times* about the inquest into the death of Elizabeth Howe. Now he sketched out a letter to a senior Member of Parliament. That, he hoped, would be the final nail in the coffin of university jurisdiction over the women of Cambridge and the dreaded Spinning House.

However, the Right Honourable Sir George Grey, Secretary of State, didn't need a report of the proceedings – although he got one. Newspapers all over the country scooped up the story. 'We doubt if any prison in England be worse managed than this,' rang the headlines of many newspapers.

But Cooper did put eager pen to official paper. He questioned Sir George about the ancient power of proctors to 'apprehend, without warrant, suspected prostitutes who were not guilty of disorderly and indecent conduct'.

The liberal-minded Grey, not a friend of the class system, had his doubts. He wrote to the vice chancellor, voicing his option that the arrest of Elizabeth Howe had been a grave mistake. He made it clear he was appalled at 'the bad management and discreditable conditions of the prison called the Spinning House'. Why, he wanted to know, had the harmful conditions 'repeatedly stated by the Inspector of Prisons, not seen any material improvement?'

Letters between Grey, Cooper and the vice chancellor passed backward and forward until March 1847. Yet, the university had no intention of relinquishing the power they held over the women of Cambridge. New regulations for the management of the Spinning House were debated and approved – a strategic gesture to quieten dissenting voices. Grey's suggestion that a matron replace the male keeper was disregarded.

But Wilson did not escape censure. Grey pointed out that it was 'unlawful for the Keeper of the Prison to sell provisions to the prisoners under his charge'. It had to stop – and it did. The testimony of six shy young women had not been entirely in vain.

Back in Cambridge, the day after the inquest, Mrs Howe prepared to return her daughter's body to Fulbourn, to be buried close to the unmarked mounds of Fenland earth under which three of her sisters already lay. She was probably unaware of the nationwide horror induced by her daughter's death. We don't know if Mrs Howe understood Mr Newby when he revealed in court that during the post-mortem of her daughter he'd discovered 'the ovaria on the left side enlarged, and on cutting it open it was found to contain a foetus'. Yet, Elizabeth had been at home in Fulbourn for the last six months. We cannot know who the father might have been, but the unborn child was another loss to the Howe family.

Musings on the Untimely Death of Elizabeth Howe

As printed in *Cambridge Independent Press*, 26 December 1846, p.4.

Poor, hapless girl! what human heart bleeds not
At all the horrors of they bitter lot!
So young – so fragile – and so doom'd to be
The victim of neglect and misery.
My faith forbids – now thy poor soul is fled,
To offer prayer – we may not for the dead;
Or Christian pity would have bent my knee
To sue for pardon, erring girl! for thee.

As now thy soul sin-laden trembling stands;
Before thy judge, awaiting his commands;
But all is bared in His Omnuiscent sight,
'Shall not the judge of all the earth do right?'

He blotteth out transgressions crimson dye,
As cloud on cloud floats o'er the azure sky;
He flings His own bright robe (without a taint)
O'er the lose sinner, and he leaves a saint.

No humans aid can aught avail thee now,
In meek submission we and only bow;
Nought an we render but the pitying tear,
Which falls spontaneous on thy lowly bier.

But thy sad mother! We may pray that she
May be supported in her grief for thee;
May be directed to the mighty rock
That opens freely to the sinners knock.

And we may pray the deep and fervent prayer
That this may warn the erring to beware;
Speak trumpet-tongued to every thoughtless breast
And godly sorrow be on each imprest.

Eliza's fate an awful warning brings.
And heaven -born pity in our bosom springs
Alas, alas, that such a tale should be
Stamp't and recorded of humanity.

D——— D ————, December 22. H.K.
[author unknown]

5

THE SPECIAL
CORRESPONDENT

In the summer of 1850, a letter arrived at 55 Albany Street, Regent's Park, London. It was the home of Mr Henry Mayhew, social reformer, co-founder of *Punch Magazine* and author of a series of books – *London Labour and the London Poor*. He was also 'special correspondent' for the popular London newspaper, the *Morning Chronicle* – a newspaper regarded as being the enemy of the class system.

Mayhew was an unconventional man. He thrived on conceiving enthusiastic ideas – he once almost blew up his house while trying to manufacture artificial diamonds. Yet, his meticulous research into the plight of the poor and fabled talent for extracting secrets from secretive people singled him out as the person most likely to galvanise the flagging outrage about the untimely death of Elizabeth Howe.

The letter, an elegant entreaty for his help, was signed by a group of 'respectable inhabitants' from Cambridge. The invisible hand of Charles Henry Cooper had been at work.

The vice chancellor hadn't taken kindly to the list of penal reforms urged by Lord Grey, Secretary of State. No matron was employed, nor were funds found to counter the cold and relentless damp seeping into every corner of the detested building. Although the keeper was forbidden to sell food and a sheet of revised rules and regulations appeared on the walls of the prison, few read them. But Cooper was anxious to see them. He wanted evidence that things had been done to improve the lives of inmates – he suspected they hadn't.

It was early autumn when the grumbling rattle of wheels turning, the creak of horses' harnesses and noise from street sellers blurred in the ears of Henry Mayhew as he strode along St Andrew's Street in search of the Spinning House, whose inhabitants would provide him with some scandalous stories for an article soon to appear in the *Morning Chronicle*. A month before, the vice chancellor had ignored Mayhew's request for a copy of the new rules and regulations. Undeterred, he turned to Cooper for archival information about the Spinning House. He told him that Thomas Hobson, a local philanthropist, donated the building – known initially as Hobson's Workhouse – for the use of the town and university to teach the poor to spin flax and earn an honest living. But Mayhew was shocked to find that much had changed since that joyful day in July 1628 when Hobson called for 'God's mercy and blessings' upon the charitable cause. The building was now used as a receptacle for disorderly women who had been committed by the vice chancellor.

Arriving at the Spinning House, Mayhew was confronted with what he later described as a 'vision of unmistakable neglect'. It sat, squat, solid and unadorned. Its ancient stonework that had once gazed over fields speckled with blossom was now cramped between tall buildings, offering a less picturesque vista.

Raising a gloved hand, he delivered a sharp knock on the prison doors as he wondered what horrors he might find inside. Wilson, the keeper, creaked the door open just enough to peer into the rotund face of the visitor. 'Tailoring?' Wilson enquired, thinking the man required the services of the business he ran to make ends meet.

'I have come to carry out a tour of the building,' Mayhew replied.

Wilson's demeanour hinted at annoyance at being troubled by someone wishing to rummage round 'his' prison. If he hadn't judged Mayhew to be 'his better', he wouldn't have admitted him and agreed to show him round.

'The cells are over two floors. Outside is a yard for exercise,' Wilson curtly explained as they began the tour.

On inspecting the exercise yard, Mayhew found a small triangle of land to the rear of the prison, enclosed by high walls and iron gates. The yard was pinched in by tall houses. Air barely had room to circulate.

Next on the tour were the cells. 'I'd like to measure the cells.' Mayhew took a measure from a large bag. Boredom turned Wilson's face to a blank canvas.

Taking out a notebook, Mayhew recorded that the cells measured 6ft by 8ft. Each was furnished with an iron bedstead, a straw mat, a flock bed, two blankets and a counterpane. There were no glazed windows in the cell. Light came through an aperture measuring about 3in square, set in iron shutters that were placed on the outside of the window frames.

'How are the cells heated?' he asked.

Sensitive to the question, Wilson explained, 'When the beds have not been slept in for some time, my servant airs them with the warming pan. The beds are good quality, Sir,' he reassured. 'There is a fire in the day room,' he added, as if to highlight the luxury he afforded his prisoners.

As he was guided along the cold, limewashed corridors, Mayhew noticed that the new rules and regulations, denied him by the vice chancellor, were pasted up on the walls. Mayhew wrote them down in his notebook:

Every person on her committal shall be required to bathe and put on a clean dress provided for her.

She shall occupy a separate cell.

Each inmate shall be provided with employment and the means of moral and religious instruction.

She will be frequently visited by the Matron, Chaplain and Medical officer.

Divine service and prayers shall be offered daily.

Doors of the cells are to be locked at 8pm and unlocked at 8am during November to February. In the other months unlocking is at 7am.

Inmates are not allowed friends without consent and then the meeting can only last a quarter of an hour and in the presence of an officer of the house.

Well conducted inmates may be selected and employed to assist in the kitchen and stores and help clean the house.

He wasn't sure who read the rules, but he discovered that they only misled the unwary as to the real character of the place. It was as though the new rules had been formulated only to placate the Secretary of State.

'I'd like to see the bathroom,' Mayhew said.

Wilson led Mayhew to the kitchen.

'Where's the tub?' Mayhew asked.

Wilson jerked his head in the direction of a metal barrel standing in the corner of the room. It was not a bath.

As Mayhew noted his findings, Wilson became restless. Suddenly, he blurted out, 'I've business to attend to!' and darted off.

'Ah,' thought Mayhew, 'away to attend to tailoring ...' He paused to reread a report contained in a letter from Cooper, detailing the findings of two prison inspectors in 1847. 'The place is damp and cold,' they had written. 'The purpose of the prison is only useful for saving a few young collegians from moral decline as the confinement of the women had no effect except to keep them off the streets during term time,' the inspectors had concluded. Mayhew was beginning to agree.

Free to roam, Mayhew snooped with glee. Through him a narrow corridor beyond the kitchen, the sound of women's voices reached him. He hurried to its source.

'Look at 'im,' nudged one of the women, as the portly, bald, 40-year-old, bumbling kind of man appeared in the prison day room. Here was the treasure Mayhew had been searching for.

'Morning ladies,' he introduced himself. 'Can I warm myself?' he asked; already, the cold and damp of the prison was creeping into his own joints.

The women eyed him up and down. His worn, yet good clothing set him apart from the gowned men who usually came into the prison. They found a chair for him.

'Thank you,' he said as he eased himself among the women, who were tightly wrapped in warm shawls. 'How do you fare in here?' he asked.

Glances around the room confirmed this man could be trusted. 'We call it going to college,' one said, amid peals of laughter.

Apparently, innocent girls blushed at the bad language of the old-timers, leaving with a new vocabulary. 'We teach 'em our ways,' laughed another. ''Tis an education.'

It was clear to Mayhew that some of the women brought into the Spinning House were innocent of the crime for which they had been arrested, or if they were guilty, they were not hardened prostitutes, just women desperate to buy food or pay the rent. Yet, the taint of the association permanently marred their chances of finding respectable employment.

As the women's stories unfolded, Mayhew struggled in his haste to scribble down every word, as so often he just wanted to stop and listen. No stranger to prison buildings and prison life, he thought this was one of the most wretched and miserable places he had ever seen.

'That Keeper, he's a busy man. He's jailer, cook, attendant, porter, chaplain and witness against us,' one said.

'Witness against you?' queried Mayhew.

'Oh yes. If he says you've been in before or been trouble you gets a longer sentence,' explained one of the women.

'He carries on as a tailor too,' chipped in another. ''Tis common knowledge.'

Correspondents to the *Cambridge Independent* had previously written that if the university wasn't prepared to pay the keeper a suitable wage, perhaps they should give up the prison and leave the improvement of the town's morals to the police force.

The women were unanimous in damning the Spinning House as a 'wretched dark, damp, filthy place that was badly managed'. 'I came in with my last little boy,' said one. 'He was three months old; he is nearly three years now and nothing inside has changed.'

This information shocked Mayhew. He'd seen the insides of many prisons, but this place was the worst. Worse because it didn't seem to be regulated in any way. The arbitrary power of the keeper was unknown in any other prison.

The tales of cruelty got worse. Despite the women's humour, it was clear there was little to laugh about.

'When I kicked up a row once, they put me in a large cell on the top row and kept me there for three days and nights without any bed to lie upon – nothing but the bare floor.'

'What had you done?' Mayhew asked.

'Well, I threw the stale bread he offered me in his face. Must have hurt him. Was so dry,' the woman proudly sniggered. 'But I wasn't eating such stale stuff as that,' she said. 'When they took [arrested] me in the street I refused to go quietly. They tore nearly everything off me. I have seen girls dragged by their hair from the day room to their cell for not keeping quiet.'

The keeper, another prisoner revealed, referred to them as his 'canaries'. They, in turn, called the cells their 'cages'.

Another 'canary' recalled that once, while she waited in her cell for the keeper to take her to the vice chancellor, he told her, 'If you go quiet, I will do all I can for you before the vice chancellor.' But when she got inside the room, he lowered his voice and said, 'Now, you wretch, you shall have all I can ever make him give you.'

He had the power, as did the Bulldogs, who claimed an intimate knowledge of the reputation of all the local women, despite their errors. Wilson and the Bulldogs played a huge part in influencing the vice chancellor's verdict. An unkind version of the truth could easily slip from the lips of their accusers if a girl had been bothersome in any way.

On one occasion, a girl was so enraged by the keeper's lies, she seized the inkstand sitting on the desk beside the vice chancellor and hurled it at the smug keeper. 'I got put into the dark hole for that,' she confessed to Mayhew. 'The next morning, I gave him what for. So, he moved me to a cell telling me it was haunted by a man who'd cut his throat.'

The women dragged inside might have been following a 'vocation', but they were punished more harshly than in any other town or prison in the country. It was clear to Mayhew that the keeper went about his business untroubled by enquiry from those who employed him.

'Evening prayers – they don't happen,' said another. It turned out that at the same time Wilson was due to be reading prayers, he was also expected to be ready at the front door, in case the proctor and his men arrived with new prisoners. Although he was a man of many talents, Wilson could not carry out his duty as porter and chaplain simultaneously. The fact that there were over 5,000 arrests between 1823, when the university took over the Spinning House, and 1853, when the place briefly closed for refurbishment, shows the keeper was indeed a very busy man.

'When they arrest you, what happens?' Mayhew asked.

'They take you to the "cage", put you in a bed. There's no light or seat. Sometimes the governor or his servant come with a warming pan.'

'We don't get supper that first night,' volunteered another. 'We are kept in the cell till about nine o'clock the next morning when the governor comes to take us to the vice chancellor's room.'

'Now, let us hear what the proctor has got to say about this,' mimicked one.

Joining the fun, several women cooed together, 'Well, Sir, I was walking down such a such street and I saw this girl and I think she is an improper character.' Peals of giggles egged on the other women.

'Did she come quiet?' the girls sang out the vice chancellor's words.

'Very quiet indeed,' would be the proctor's reply. Unless, of course, a struggle had taken place.

'And then you get to speak?' asked Mayhew.

'No. Then a paper is signed and given to the governor, who takes us back to our cells.'

The treatment of women arrested on suspicion and their committal without evidence showed, Mayhew thought, a worse than inefficient, unjust system. It was clear to him that the once benevolent Hobson's charity had been completely diverted from its original aims.

The form of trial the women faced after their arrest was, Mayhew wrote in his report, 'repugnant to every principle of justice as it is opposed to the notions English customs and English liberties'. He concluded that Cambridge was stifled by tradition and the prejudice of a social elite.

The students and their masters all came from backgrounds where women were homemakers or whores. Unmarried, working-class women existed solely for their own amusement. No wonder riots broke out on the streets of Cambridge when sisters, wives and sweethearts were routinely ruined by incarceration inside the dreaded Spinning House.

In January 1851, the much-anticipated article based on his visit to Cambridge appeared in the *Morning Chronicle*. It was entitled 'The Spinning House Abomination', and was swiftly duplicated in the *Cambridge Independent*, filling several tall column inches of dense black print. They were copied again. This time reprinted as a pamphlet, *The Spinning House Abomination*, which was eagerly snapped up by local readers.

I eagerly devoured this 'souvenir edition', now elegantly bound in a dark blue cover, its title spelt out in tiny gold lettering. While reading the shocking details, I imagined the gossip it must have generated at the time, the whispering of women asking if their friends had read it. Would it have been 'respectable' to admit to having devoured every word? I wondered how it might have divided the town between those who shunned its salacious words and those who were fired up to demand that their elected members do more to end the suffering.

Cooper was correct in thinking that the printed words of an outsider could strike a heavier blow than fists ever could. It was, however, Queen Victoria's husband who would, indirectly, strike the next blow.

6

THE MEMORIAL

An autumnal wind blew dancing leaves along the street as William Henry Apthorpe walked towards the home of Charles Henry Cooper in Jesus Lane. Both men were preparing for a difficult discussion, one which they knew could explode in anger. Apthorpe covered the half-mile distance at an angry pace, yet the damp chill of a mid-November evening did not cool his burning fury. He was one of the men behind the letter requesting Henry Mayhew's assistance in denouncing the Spinning House. He had good reason.

Both men were active members of Cambridge Liberal Association. Apthorpe was the Liberal Member for East Barnwell. A man respected, and vilified in some quarters, for being a 'friend of the working man'. He had made it clear on election that he would not shrink from championing the rights of the town over the university. It was Apthorpe who had fought for a healthier drainage system in Barnwell – whose population easily succumbed to fatal illnesses.

But respect had been in short supply, a few evenings before, when his wife and daughter fell under the odious suspicion of a proctor. He was a townsman seeking revenge.

The timing of Apthorpe's visit was pertinent for Cooper, who had just discovered he wasn't the only man striving for reform in Cambridge. When, in 1847, Prince Albert, the Prince Consort, became Chancellor of Cambridge University, he'd immediately noticed Britain lagged behind the universities of his native Germany – who had made great progress in teaching modern sciences to equip students for the modern age.

If the elite educational establishments of the prince's adopted country were to rival their European cousins, urgent reforms were needed. So, in 1850, Albert set up a royal commission to review the studies, discipline and finances of the ancient universitates of Oxford, Cambridge and Dublin. The news had fallen on the welcome ears of Cooper, who thought the more the commissioners delved into the running of the university, the more it would be discovered that collegiate revenues could be used to increase the number of lecture rooms and scientific laboratories.

As Apthorpe settled into a comfortable seat beside a blazing fire in Cooper's study, an exhalation of pent-up emotions escaped his tense body as he paused to calm himself before painting the scene that kept spinning round his head for several days. 'A few of nights ago,' Apthorpe found the words were hard to speak at first, 'I was walking in Trumpington Street with my wife and daughter. I'd fallen behind, stopped to talk to a friend. I didn't see the proctor and his men were close. As I moved to catch up with my family I looked ahead. I was shocked at what I saw. My wife and daughter were in the grip of a proctor and his Bulldogs.'

Cooper had heard whispered gossip about what had happened that night and knew Apthorpe sought vengeance.

'Tears were falling down my daughter's face. My wife seemed unsteady. I feared she would faint.' Apthorpe bowed his head, choking out that the proctor had not only stopped his wife and daughter, but he'd laid hands on them – an unimaginable insult.

The indignity and fear of being stopped and questioned by men searching for prostitutes could not be underestimated. Idle gossip was the enemy of any woman.

'I escorted the women to a place of safety,' Apthorpe continued, 'and returned to find the proctor. I wanted an apology.'

Anger coursed through Apthorpe as he related what happened next. 'He refused. He claimed he'd not touched my daughter. Only looked under her bonnet.' Apthorpe spat the words and pummelled his thighs with clenched fists. 'I don't know how I didn't strike that odious man,' he confessed.

Cooper knew fists and fights wouldn't end the privileges of the proctors to harass and arrest women. Cunning was needed. But first, he must calm Apthorpe.

He had an idea. 'I wonder if the royal commissioners are acquainted with the words written by Mayhew in *The Spinning House Abomination?*' Cooper took a sideways swerve to tempt his friend with an idea he believed could end the proctors' powers.

'I doubt it?' Apthorpe wasn't sure where this was going.

'What if …' Cooper's words were slow but precise. 'What if Prince Albert's commissioners were to receive a Memorial – a petition – from the Borough Council demanding an end to the ancient rights and privileges of the university that cause so much offence.'

'All they do is cause trouble on the streets,' Apthorpe said. But he wasn't sure members would agree to such a bold action. Not every elected member had the interests of the town in mind when seeking re-election, and anyway, would they dare? Every year, every elected member of the council had to attend the Magna Congregatio, or Black Assembly, to swear obedience to the university to maintain their privileges and laws.

The social and economic gains of siding with the university could not be overestimated. Opposing them could be ruinous. Yet, the bickering between town and gown about who should pay for what was exasperating the townspeople, who longed for a modern supply of clean water and the efficient disposal of its wastewater. The River Cam was already an open sewer. And they wanted to know that their women folk were free to walk unmolested in the streets.

'It's time to end proctorial authority over people who aren't members of the university.' Cooper's words flowed forcefully; he was in campaigning mood. 'The laws and privileges of the university, deemed acceptable centuries before, are obsolete in a town whose population had tripled over the past fifty years,' he said – it now stood at 27,000. 'Rules suiting 800 part-time resident members of the university, living in spacious airy courts, when the rest of the population are pressed into cramped yards inside the boundary of the old medieval town, are obsolete in a modern world.'

The royal commissioners, tasked by the prince to modernise the university, were stirring the stagnant waters lurking behind the stone walls of the Cambridge colleges. But requests for ancient documents and founding deeds had been met with petulant inactivity. Yet Cooper, who'd consulted them for his *Annals*, knew their hiding places. He could aid the prince in his determined effort to force senior members of the university to do more than sit in their rooms, eat dinners, go to chapel, read books, consume large quantities of alcohol and otherwise amuse themselves. It was a suggestion that appalled many of the fossilised fellows clinging to monastic traditions – although this was exactly what many younger college men wanted.

The wheels of inertia propelling Cambridge University backward, rather than forward, are legendary even today. Growing up in Cambridge, I often wondered why the railway station, opened in 1845, had been built a mile out of town. The reason turned out to be because it was delayed as university officials negotiated the precise wording of the 1844 Cambridge Railway Act. Exacting clauses prevented students from travelling without the written permission of their tutor – ticket sellers could be fined for disobeying the rule. Such was the fear that the railway would transport 'shoals of bad women' into town that weekend travel was heavily restricted.

The unbridled power of the university over the townspeople was beginning to grate. In April 1846, the same year bloody riots had broken out on the streets of Cambridge in protest about the number of women being thrown into the Spinning House, Spencer Luke Nightingale, tailor and robe maker, was summoned to the Vice Chancellor's Court for taking legal proceedings against a student owing him money. His crime was not having first given notice of his intention to the student's tutor.

The vice chancellor punished him in the usual way. He was 'discommuned'. The vice chancellor issued an order forbidding all members of university from directly, or indirectly, having any dealings whatsoever with Nightingale. Four months later, Nightingale appeared in the bankruptcy courts in London – a broken man.

I was shocked to discover the system of 'discommuning' was abolished only in 1971.

The glowing fire in Cooper's study, and detectable in his flicking eyes, reassured Apthorpe. Cunning was required.

'I must stay in the background,' Cooper said. 'I must appear neutral.' After all, as town clerk it was his duty to remain neutral. It was his job to enact decisions made by the town council, not rouse them towards treason!

Apthorpe did the sums in his head, calculating that just enough councillors could be swayed in the right direction. 'We can count on our Liberal friends,' he said.

The two men didn't realise they were about to hatch a plan that would end with an Act of Parliament.

Having so recently researched and published his *Annals*, Cooper understood the ancient charters serving the interests of the university, as opposed to those of the town, better than anyone alive. Between them, Apthorpe and Cooper selected eighteen 'rules' – there were a great many more – causing the greatest social and economic damage to the town. The right to arrest and imprison women suspected of soliciting was top of the list.

A series of clandestine meetings with liberal-minded councillors took place until the pair were confident of a majority vote.

On Friday, 6 February 1852, the town council convened with the intention of finalising the wording of the memorial destined for the royal commissioners. A draft copy had been circulated in advance of the meeting. Now, at four o'clock in the afternoon, as twenty-eight town councillors took their places in the Council Chamber of the Town Hall, in the same seats that university officials had assuredly occupied during the inquest of Elizabeth Howe, the ancient authority of the university was about to unravel.

As Cooper gazed out of a window overlooking the Market Square, he recalled not only the chilling testimony of the young women giving evidence against the Spinning House keeper, Mr Wilson, some six years before, but also the anguish of Mrs Howe upon learning of the slow and painful death of her daughter. He hoped that day would conclude years of protest and anger about the tyranny of the university. But that afternoon, one councillor was determined to do his utmost to obstruct or delay the ratifying of the document. In a place that bred class warfare, where allegiances were scrutinised, sides taken and those pleasing the 'right' people prospered, it was never going to be easy to win the day.

Roland Morris Fawcett had been appointed by the university as surgeon of the Spinning House, and at the time of Elizabeth Howe's death, he had written to the *Cambridge Chronicle* placing all the blame in the irresponsible hands of the young woman's friends. They should have sought medical assistance sooner, he had chided. He had little thought for the subsequent bill. He had little thought for the welfare of the women placed in the Spinning House.

'We must be mindful of not upsetting our powerful neighbour, from which two hundred thousand pounds a year flow into the town,' he was quick to warn. 'It is vital the proctors remove suspicious women from the streets. Remember, the police lack the authority to arrest women on grounds of suspicion,' he cautioned. 'Oh yes,' he went on, 'mistakes were made', but they were trivial and few. What did it matter when it was for the greater good of 'protecting fine young men from temptation'?

'Parents,' someone else spoke up in support of Fawcett, 'look to the proctors to protect their sons' morals.'

'It causes anger,' a councillor claimed. 'I have known ladies belonging to the most respectable families in this town, daughters and wives of professional men, men of position and of family – not tradesmen or college servants – stopped and insulted in the most gross and offensive manner,' he reminded the room. A fact Apthorpe knew too well.

The dry voice of Cooper was heard. 'The right to arrest women only deceives parents into thinking the proctors can control prostitution in Cambridge. There is no evidence the Spinning House deters prostitution, but it does cause ill feeling when innocent victims are insulted and wrongly arrested.'

The next grievance appearing on the memorial that Cooper and Apthorpe had compiled was discussed. It was the enforced attendance at the Magna Congregatio, an event requiring town officials to swear to accept laws and privileges benefitting the gown – but not always the town.

'What does it matter if we have to come here once a year to bow before the vice chancellor?' Fawcett tried to trivialise a ceremony that was loathed by many.

The groans and hisses, aimed at Fawcett's attempts to defend his masters, grew louder as he battled on to defend every point listed on the memorial. They included objections to the right of the vice chancellor to license alehouses and the sale of wine and spirits, and the control of weights and measures; his punishment of tradesmen who exceeded the £5 credit limit imposed on students – known as 'discommuning' and ensuring their ruin. He controlled the giving of licences for theatres and entertainment in the town. In fact, any activity which might tempt a scholar from his studies was jealously regulated, and those flouting it were punished. Fawcett justified them all as being vital to protect young men fresh from the guiding hand of parents or schoolmasters.

'We must delay,' Fawcett demanded, 'and have a conference with the university.'

'No, no!' came a chorus of annoyance.

Most in the room were familiar with the delaying tactic so often used by the university and its supporters to stall irritating demands from the town. With senior members of the university and its scholars only resident for twenty-four weeks a year, finding time for a conference with its officials always managed to dilute its urgency.

As the afternoon moved to evening the men's stomachs began to growl for their dinners, so the mayor proposed a vote on the wording of the document, so they could all get home. Despite Fawcett's passionate defence, twenty-two were in favour of the wording, four against and two abstained. The memorial, with its eighteen demands, was agreed, sealed and sent to the royal commissioners the following day. Cooper and Apthorpe relished the moment.

The memorial arrived on the desk of the royal commissioners in no time at all, but three years of acrimony followed. The town refused to back down on any point; the university did the same. But the university knew that conditions inside the Spinning House could prove embarrassing if the commissioners demanded its scrutiny. It was time for the university to enact the suggestions, urged by Sir George Grey, Secretary of State, following the inquest into the death of Elizabeth Howe.

In August 1852, Charles Henry Cooper, as town clerk, was privy to an interesting piece of information, which he was eager to share with Apthorpe. The fire flickered in the grate of Cooper's study that summer's day. A refreshing breeze from an open window soothed the brows of the two men as they ruminated on the memorial's stalemate.

'They [he was referring to the university] plan to refurbish the Spinning House,' he announced. 'Today, I have been instructed to place an advertisement in the *Chronicle* requesting tenders for the work.'

On 4 November 1853, the newly refurbished Spinning House received an illustrious visitor. Joseph Romilly, university registrar and famous diarist (he kept detailed records of his academic life), knocked on its door. He wanted to make a written record of the benevolence of the university in updating the ancient building.

Each cell, he reported, now boasted its own gaslight, three-legged stool and a bell. A stove had been installed, 'which heats the whole building,' he claimed. The Inspector of Prisons had visited, he wrote, and 'expressed complete satisfaction' with the work. But one thing, or rather person, that did not impress Romilly was Wilson, the keeper, who he described as 'not quite sober and had an extravagant opinion of his own merits' and who ran a tailoring business from the premises.

News of Romilly's inspection had useful consequences. Later that month, the *Morning Post*, whose special correspondent Henry Mayhew had taken a great interest in the Spinning House when he had written *The Spinning House Abomination* a few years earlier, informed his readers that the university, 'having obtained advice and counsel from the inspector of prisons had agreed to dispense with a male Keeper'. In future, a matron and an assistant would live on the premises. Their pay would allow them to devote their whole time to their duties.

But had the university done enough to persuade its critics, and especially the royal commissioners, of its continued right to run its private prison?

In 1855, Sir John Patterson, a 65-year-old retired and partially deaf judge prized for his clear and decisive judgments, was appointed to arbitrate between the town and gown. Immediately, he sent for Charles Henry Cooper, the only man to fully understand the ancient laws and charters of the university.

For four days that February, and four more the following May, Sir John listened to arguments from both sides. Then he retired to his country home in Devon to deliberate on 'the long and complicated mass of details'. It was 31 August when he took up his pen to disclose the outcome of these deliberations.

The Vice Chancellor of Cambridge University and the Mayor of Cambridge both sat in their respective corners of the town to read the outcome of Patterson's deliberations.

The Magna Congregatio was considered outdated. No longer would the mayor and councillors be required to swear to 'conserve the liberties and privileges of the University of Cambridge'. He upheld the university's right to discommune tradesmen – to protect profligate students, he wrote. No change was made to the licensing of theatrical performances, except those taking place during the long vacation.

He amended certain complicated tax loopholes that had previously favoured the university. Any money the council gained in tax revenue, however, was quickly lost, as Sir John stipulated that both sides must pay an equal share of the costs incurred to resolve the matter – which amounted to £2,000. This was £1,000 that could have gone towards providing clean water, a sewage system and modern municipal buildings in Cambridge.

Perhaps the most disappointing decision – certainly for Councillor Apthorpe – was that the proctors retained the right to arrest and detain women because 'where a considerable part of the population consists of young men at a very critical time of life with strong passions and little self-control, must have paid off as the Spinning House was deemed a hospitable place to detain young women'. The revamp had had its desired result – for some.

In 1856, the Cambridge University Act was passed. It was long and detailed and brought together revisions suggested by the royal commissioners and those contained in the town council's memorial. There was no clear winner, but at least the town had been liberated from the galling, inferior position of having to swear to maintain the rights and privileges of the university. It was a start.

By then, the untimely death of Elizabeth Howe was only a memory, yet it had triggered freedoms for the townspeople and some long-awaited improvement to the Spinning House. The university, however, was still free to harass and imprison women.

But public opinion was about to force even further change.

7

THE BACHELORS' BALL

Emma (Emily) Kemp

Age: 24

Arrested: 30 January 1860

Arresting proctor: The Reverend Mr Wollaston

Charge: Being a loose and disorderly woman found in the company of members of the university

Sentence: Fourteen days

In November 1859 it was announced that the date of the Bachelor of Arts (BA) exams was to be changed. At the time, it seemed an unremarkable decision, something of interest only to scholars. The move, however, triggered dramatic events, culminating in a young dressmaker challenging the Vice Chancellor of Cambridge University in one of the highest courts in the land, in a battle to defend her untarnished reputation.

A spite-ridden letter from a jealous rival sparked the sorrowful turn of events that led to 24-year-old Emma Kemp paying a heavy price for the catty prose of an anonymous foe.

When news of the change of date for the BA exams trickled along the narrow streets and yards of Cambridge, gossip and speculation were rife. Would this lead to the cancellation of the annual Bachelors' Ball? This eagerly awaited society occasion was always held at the end of January to celebrate the conferment of BA degrees.

The ball contributed to the coffers of the town, too. Each year, over 400 members of Cambridge's elite society, from the university, the town and county, gathered to enjoy the delight that was the Bachelors' Ball. Titled men, their wives, daughters and the proud young graduates packed into the Town Hall for an enchanting evening of merriment. Under the watchful eye of parents and proctors, young men and women of rank danced and sipped fine wine. Such vigilance steered highly respectable young ladies into the paths of fine, educated men about to embark on their adult lives.

Dressmakers gathered outside the Town Hall to glimpse the latest fashions. To watch a world they could only dream of belonging to. Inside hung the colourful flags of college rowing clubs and garlands of red and blue ribbons decorated the walls. Dancers spun and turned in gallops and quadrilles while a band of distinction played till dawn in rooms perfumed with foliage and flowers specially selected for the occasion. A magnificent supper was served in time to reinvigorate the fatigued. An invitation to such a ball marked out those favoured by the university, and those in its favour easily endorsed those who enhanced their social and economic standing.

Already, that November of 1859, the prospect of the ball had stirred excitement among the stylish inhabitants of the town, who'd booked their places at Miss Stainton's Dance School, where private tuition in the 'newest and most fashionable' dances of the season was promised. Only those of distinction were invited to apply for her exclusive tuition.

So, when news filtered through that the ball was to be cancelled, it came as a heavy blow. Not wanting to disappoint the titled ladies to whom many had already pledged a dance, twelve very well-connected Trinity students hastily formed an organising committee. They couldn't allow an administrative adjustment to spoil their fun. A large room at the Lion Hotel – a smaller venue than the Town Hall – was booked and 200 invitations were sent out.

However, one young man, 21-year-old William Graham of Emmanuel College, was not on the guest list. He, too, had been looking forward to celebrating at the famous ball, but now all he could do was read newspaper reports of the Trinity Men's 'fashionable gathering', held on Thursday, 8 December. He learnt that Messrs Moyes caterers had provided a lavish supper and that the Coote & Tinney Quadrille Band had kept noblemen, masters of colleges, undergraduates and their ladies on the dance floor until four in the morning.

Taking inspiration from the determined Trinity students, Graham decided to follow their example. He found another dozen BA men eager to dance and dine – although not as well endowed with stately connections as the original party planners – who devised a plan for their own scaled-down version of the Trinity Ball. Graham, the eldest son of the Vicar of Hinxton, a village about 8 miles outside Cambridge, was the perfect person to know where to find premises suitable for a private dance.

To avoid the prying eyes of the proctors, who, he knew, would not look favourably on the spree, he booked a room at the De Freville Arms Inn in Shelford, a village 4 miles to the south of Cambridge. He ordered a supper, booked musical entertainment and arranged an omnibus to take himself, his younger brother, the band and some dancing partners to and from Shelford on the evening of 30 January 1860 – the customary date for the Bachelors' Ball.

Printed invitations were not issued. Secrecy was essential. The proctors must not know of the plan. As these young men did not have an easy list of sisters and cousins they could invite to such a secret ball, they needed to find suitable young ladies willing to accompany them. Graham already knew the girl he wanted to invite.

William Graham had first noticed the pretty bonneted face of Emma Kemp at the Grand Monster Fete held at Fenner's cricket ground the previous July. The ticket for this thrilling event promised a daring tightrope dance by the famed Madame Genevie and the glorious ascent of a gigantic hot-air balloon. The fete had been an expensive undertaking for its organisers, but the admission price of 2s, it was claimed, was within the command of all classes. By three o'clock that warm summer's afternoon, as the gates to the cricket ground swung open to welcome its guests, the sun had pushed away the dull clouds of the morning. Gaily coloured crinolines soon decorated the grass as hundreds of visitors arrived.

Determined to make the immediate acquaintance of the pretty girl he'd spotted, Graham wove his way through the crowds. 'Good afternoon.' He tipped his straw boater at the girls as he introduced himself. 'What luck with the weather,' he commented.

Already giddy under the blaze of summer skies, Emma was delighted to engage in conversation with such a charming young man. 'Sir, my name is Emma Kemp,' she said. Turning to the girl on her arm, she introduced her friend, Harriet Bell.

Graham chatted and flattered, putting the girls at ease before enquiring, 'May I accompany you to the refreshment tent?'

Emma and Harriet had been weighing up the respectability of the gentleman. A shared nod confirmed their approval of this amiable young man. Why not spend an afternoon in his company, the girls thought.

'That is kind, Sir,' Emma replied.

Soon friends, the innocent trio cried out in wonderment as they lifted their straw-hatted heads upwards to enjoy the daring tightrope dancing executed by the famed Madame Genevie. Later, they watched with nervous excitement as Mr Goddard's gigantic hot-air balloon swayed to and fro in the late afternoon breeze before flames shot up inside it in readiness for its spectacular ascent. At six o'clock, they jumped and gasped at the loud bangs and crackling colours of the fireworks signalling the end of a wonderful afternoon. It had been a perfect summer's day.

Since the fun of the fete, Emma and Graham had spotted each other several times while walking in the busy streets close to the city centre. In December 1859, their paths crossed again.

Emma was on an errand searching for the right ribbon for a dress when she noticed the smiling face of William Graham approaching her. Christmas shoppers were swelling the busy streets, forcing him to twist and turn as his made his way to her side. He steered her towards the relative calm of a doorway. He had a special request to make.

'I'm so glad to see you,' he said. 'Would you do me the honour of joining me at a ball?' The words were so easily said. 'I'm soon leaving for London to the Law.'

What a surprise. Emma was a jumble of emotions. Of course she wanted to go to a ball. In her mind, she saw herself dancing in a pretty dress, but the propriety of accepting such an invitation was another matter. And what would her mother say? Deep inside, she knew the answer to that question.

'I don't think it would be proper,' she replied as she gently pressed him for more details.

'Well, it's on a Monday, 30 January. In Shelford, at the De Freville Arms Inn. Do you know it?' he asked. 'Bring a friend if you like.'

Emma was flattered and excited by the invitation, but could she accept it? In the spirit of the moment, she promised to give him her answer in a few days.

'Keep it a secret,' he whispered as he pushed his way back through the Christmas crowds and laden carts crammed into every available space.

Emma did so want to go dancing, but caution checked her excitement.

Census records paint a picture of the precarious plight of the Kemp family. Emma's father died a few short months after her birth in August 1833. In June 1844, her widowed mother married Abraham Locker.

A half-sister, Louisa, arrived in 1846, but her father died when she was only 6 years old. With no male protector, the family lodged with their maternal grandmother in Barnwell, earning a living 'charring'.

By the time Graham met Emma, the family's dignity had been restored. The small female family was renting their own home. Emma was working as a respected milliner and dressmaker; her mother, Mrs Locker, cooked and cleaned for several prestigious families in the town. Fourteen-year-old Louisa, although still at school, contributed to the household income by taking in embroidery. Their battle for economic independence had been won. So, despite being sworn to secrecy, Emma knew if she were to accept the invitation to a ball, she must be certain it would be respectable, and she would need a chaperone.

For days, Emma turned over in her mind the rights and wrongs of accepting the invitation. Her thoughts swung between propriety and pleasure. What would her mother say? Would the dance be a respectable one? What would she wear? Could she trust the intentions of Graham?

After days of anguish, she decided to consult her friend, Harriet Bell. She'd met Graham, did she think him a gentleman? So, one Sunday afternoon as the friends ambled from Barnwell to the city centre to admire the tempting Christmas window displays in the larger shops, Emma braved breaking her promise not to tell. The two were quite possibly outside Fenner & Bowles in Market Hill, a grocer's shop which always put on an enticing display of festive luxury fruits and tempting tinned goods, when Emma turned her face towards her friend's ear. 'I've had an invitation,' Emma whispered.

'You have?' There was excitement in Harriet's voice. She had a confession too. Leaning closer, she whispered back, 'I have as well.' It was to the same event, it had to be. Such invitations were so rare.

'From William Graham?' Emma asked.

'No, a friend of his.'

'Oh, Harriet, I'm so excited!'

Did she dare to go, though? Surely if her friend was going there could be no harm in it?

'But should we go?' asked Emma. 'You don't seem at all worried.'

'Of course, you must. We must.' It was clear Harriet was determined to go.

'But what if we're found out?'

'Don't worry,' Harriet laughed. 'It's out of town. The proctors will never know. The university boys must be in their college by midnight. Everyone is sworn to secrecy.'

Harriet made the plan seem so simple. Was there any harm in it, Emma wondered? She had never known Graham to be improper. He had always treated her with respect. She enjoyed his company. If they were to be back by midnight, then Emma decided she would go to the ball. The girls would travel together, in effect, chaperoning each other.

With decency established, she agreed to accept the invitation. With smiles on their faces and excited voices that got a little louder than they might have realised, the pair discussed what they might wear, what dances they might dance, what luxuries might appear at the supper Graham had promised to order.

On the drizzly morning of Monday, 30 January, the day of the secret ball, a letter arrived at the Porters' Lodge, Trinity College. It was addressed to the Reverend Mr Blore. Clutching the letter, a college servant rushed across Great Court to Mr Blore's rooms in Nevile's Court.

First, he examined the quality of the notepaper. It was different from the stationery he usually received. Carefully, he slid the cold steel of his paper knife through the envelope, curious as to what the strange letter might contain. Reading the neatly spaced inky words, a wave of unease flooded his body. The letter revealed shocking information:

Rev. Sir, I wish to call your attention to a circumstance that came under my notice a day or two ago. I understand a ball and supper is to take place on Monday, the 30th, the party consisting of 12 young girls of the town, and 12 university men. It is arranged they should meet at 6 o'clock on Monday evening, at the new Tennis Court, at the corner of East Road, where there will be one or more omnibuses to convey them to Shelford, the place chosen for the ball.

The party is got up by Miss Emma Kemp, and an Emmanuel gentleman, a friend of hers, who has just passed the Senate and is giving this in honour of it. I hear there are to be 2 or 3 King's gentlemen, and the rest are your own men [Trinity]. I also hear a Miss Sharman in Post Office Terrace is to be one of the party. Miss Kemp lives in Dover Street, East Road. You will doubtless wonder where I got my information from.

The fact is, I used to employ Miss Kemp as she professed to get her living by dressmaking, but I have been convinced to the contrary as I have heard she has discontinued with it. She came to my house the other evening and I inquired of my servant the object of her visit. She told me Miss Kemp had been several times trying to persuade her to go to a party. I, of course, insisted upon knowing what kind of party it was when she told me what I have just stated, and more than that she added that Miss Kemp was going to take her sister, a little girl about 14 years of age.

The supper is being prepared by Mr Peeling, Benet's Street. It is to be sent over to Shelford to be taken at 10 o'clock and breakfast is ordered. I think you will find this statement perfectly correct. My husband intended calling upon you, but I thought it better to write. I trust you will use your authority as a Proctor to endeavour to put a stop to the evils that are so frequently occurring in Cambridge.

I am yours respectfully – An inhabitant of the Town

The letter could not be ignored. The proctor could not know then that some of the letter's malicious facts were a work of fiction.

First, Blore sent a servant to ascertain if supper had been ordered from Peeling's dining rooms. It had, by William Graham from Emmanuel College. The letter must therefore be taken seriously. Blore knocked on the door of another Trinity proctor, the Reverend Mr Thomas Samuel Woollaston. He sent for his Bulldogs – the special constables who assisted the proctors on their nightly patrols round the town. Had they heard of this Emma Kemp, he wanted to know? They had not.

It was decided that the vice chancellor must be informed of the plan. Gripping the letter from the 'inhabitant of the town', the pair hurried along Bridge Street, passing over the River Cam – Cambridge's busy trading and industrial heartland – onto Magdalene Street and its college, whose Master Latimer Neville was the current vice chancellor.

'Do you know this woman, Kemp?' asked Neville, meaning had she been arrested before?

'I do not,' Wollaston replied. He explained the only enquiry he had made was to ask his men if they knew the girl.

'Did they make enquiry?' Neville asked.

'I believe not,' replied Woollaston

'Well, the plan must be prevented,' a worried Neville declared, 'and this Emma Kemp brought in.'

The omnibus was due to depart Cambridge at six o'clock. The men had several hours ahead of them to plan how to prevent its cargo reaching its planned destination.

As those same minutes and hours ticked by, Emma Kemp and some two dozen other youngsters were savouring the anticipation of an evening of entertainment. On the afternoon of Monday, 30 January, Emma and her half-sister, Louisa, trod lightly as they descended the wooden stairs of their home in Dover Street, Barnwell. On their lips was a repeat of the lie they had already told their mother a few days before.

'We're off to the tea party,' Emma called out as the sisters slipped out of the house, their winter shawls concealing the pretty dresses they had chosen to wear.

'I'll be working late,' Emma's mother absently called from the back room where she was stealing a few moments' rest before going to help at a party one of her employers was holding that evening.

Having escaped unnoticed, the carried pair walked to Harriet Bull's house, a few streets away in Adam and Eve Row. Harriet was a dressmaker and milliner, her father a tailor, so it was the perfect place for the girls to gather to tweak and trim their dresses and hair, doing their very best to look like young women going to a version of the Bachelors' Ball.

It was ten minutes to six when the giggling girls stood before Harriet's 13-year-old brother. 'How do we look?'

He approved and gallantly offered to chaperone them through the semi-dark streets to where Melbourne Place joined Parker's Piece, the place the omnibus had been instructed to collect the girls and later deposit them. At the same time, a few streets away, three other girls were making their way towards the second pick-up point along the road, near the new tennis courts.

On the dot of six o'clock the sound of horses' hooves was heard. The omnibus drew up at the meeting place. On its roof, hampers stuffed full of the supper provided by Peelings had been secured, together with some musical instruments. The girls gathered up their skirts and clambered into the dimly lit interior. Already on board were Graham and his younger brother, Charles, along with 'White Headed Bob', a popular local musician, and members of his band who had been specially hired for the evening.

Next, the omnibus rattled off to collect the three girls waiting a little further along the road. Within minutes all were crowded inside. The bus jolted and began its gentle swing and clatter on its journey to Shelford. Other guests were already preparing to make their way in separate prearranged flies and gigs.

Everything had been so carefully, so secretly, arranged, yet the omnibus had barely travelled 100 yards when the driver pulled up the horses' reins, bringing the carriage to an unexpected halt. An icy, silent fear crept into the warm, beating hearts of the passengers. A voice pierced the cold night's silence. At the sound the occupants of the bus ceased, for a few seconds, to breathe.

'Are any gentlemen of the university on board?'

No one moved. No one spoke. Emma didn't know what to do. She glanced at Graham. A look of unease had replaced the happy smiles of a moment before.

Meeting her eyes, Graham woke from a trance. His gentlemanly instincts kicked in. He was the organiser and he must discover the reason for the hold-up. Stepping down the omnibus steps onto the hard surface of the road below, he readied himself for an explanation. His words never passed his lips. He froze.

It was clear to him, even in the dim light of a January evening, that the bus was at the centre of a well-planned ambush. Four proctors surrounded the vehicle. With them were four Bulldogs. A dozen or so policemen also stood firm. The highway ahead was barred.

Two policemen stepped forward to still the horses' heads. Everything had come to a menacing halt.

A proctor Graham did not recognise stepped forward. 'Name and college?'

It was Blore. 'Are there any other members of the university with you?'

Hearing this from inside, Graham's younger brother clambered out, followed by an awkward looking White Head Bob and his band, who wanted to be anywhere else than where they were at that moment. They climbed up to retrieve the instruments strapped onto the roof; they already knew they would not be using them that evening.

'Where is this bus going?' a proctor asked.

Again no one spoke.

Blore climbed up into the omnibus, peering into its dimly lit interior. What he saw confirmed his suspicions. Along the two upholstered seats, seven anxious pairs of eyes stared at him. Later, in court, he would confess he hadn't obtained a clear picture of those sitting inside the vehicle, but it was enough, he maintained, to form an opinion of their class. 'They couldn't possibly have been ladies,' he would claim, 'when the journey had started in an omnibus setting off from Barnwell.'

Under instruction from a proctor, two further police constables mounted the steps of the bus. Escape was impossible, even if the girls had had the courage to try. A command was given. The driver urged the horses on. But where was it going?

'What's happening?'

'Where are they taking us?'

These were the unanswered questions swirling around the minds of the young women. Emma put a comforting arm around her young sister. Louisa fought back tears. Tiny drops of salty water pooled in the eyes of the other girls too.

'It'll be the Spinning House!' Harriet spat out the words that all suspected.

'But we've done nothing wrong,' sobbed Louisa, losing control in the short-lived security of her sisters' arms.

'Won't matter,' Harriet muttered under her breath.

Graham suspected where the horses were being led and followed on foot. He was angry. He wanted to defend the girls. Within minutes, all arrived in front of the heavy doors of the Spinning House. The horses, once again, were drawn to a standstill.

'Out you get!' came a gruff voice.

No one moved.

'Out, I say!'

The girls were now in the inescapable grip of the proctors. Fear rendered them incapable of movement. The Bulldogs were sent in to forcibly drag each girl out of their seat.

'We've done nothing wrong!' Emma pleaded as she was pulled and shoved out of the bus and onto the hard pavement. 'My young sister is with me. She has done nothing wrong. At least let her go,' she begged.

Graham challenged one of the proctors. 'What right do you have to stop me?'

'You're not wearing your academicals. I could fine you for that,' he was told.

'The girls are all respectable,' Graham firmly stated.

'The vice chancellor will see about that,' came the harsh reply.

It was no use. He was unable to save his dancing partner. William Graham and his brother could only watch in despair as seven frightened young women were swallowed up in the bleak darkness as the heavy gates of the dreaded Spinning House closed behind them.

The brothers were ordered back to their college. As he walked the short distance to Emmanuel College, Graham wondered, given all the secrecy, how the proctors had found out about the ball. It would be almost a year later when, in a courtroom at Westminster Hall, London, the spiteful truth about that evening would be revealed. Although no one would ever know the identity of the cruel correspondent.

Dragged from the shelter of the omnibus, Emma and the other frightened girls huddled together in the inner yard of the Spinning House.

A wintery damp was already creeping through their party clothes. Only Harriet Bell had ever entered the place before, a fact she remained silent about, although the matron, Mrs Agnes Johnson, who'd replaced the crooked keeper – Wilson – thought she recognised Bell.

It had been four years since the capable Mrs Johnson had taken charge of the Spinning House. An ex-matron of Durham Prison, her testimonials had been glowing; she was even described as 'quite a treasure'. So much had been in a muddle under Wilson but gone now were all his swindling tricks, exposed to all during the inquest into the death of Elizabeth Howe.

Matron took each of the girls' names. She needed to consult the Committal Books before the vice chancellor arrived to question the new prisoners. She found no written record of the arrest of any of the girls, yet suspicion clung to Harriet's name.

Emma drew Louisa close to her while they anxiously waited. 'I'll protect you,' she whispered. But each girl was separated as, one by one, they were taken into a small, whitewashed room where the stern eyes and terse voices of four proctors pierced through each forlorn girl. The same questions were fired at them.

'What is your name and occupation?'

'Have you been here before?'

'Who are your parents?'

'Where were you going?'

'Who was in charge?'

The first interrogation lasted minutes. Then Matron escorted the prisoners to their cells. Each girl was stunned into silence as she was led along narrow, dimly lit corridors, haunted by restless shadows, until they reached the cell block. The twenty-three cells were arranged over two floors; the stark black of their cold doors shone in the pale light. But it was the sound of keys turning in locks that confirmed to each of the seven young women the bleak consequences of that evening's escapade.

There was no fireplace in the bare brick of the cell walls, no covering on the equally bare brick floor. Tiny wisps of invisible air caused the jet of gaslight, permitted only at certain times, to throw dark shapes into every corner of the room. None of the former partygoers had any idea how long they would be shut in.

An hour passed. Emma, locked in her cell, became anxious for news of her sister. It was a long time since Louisa had been forced from her arms to follow Matron to the small whitewashed room for questioning.

Now she scolded herself. Why had she been such a fool? How would she face her mother? Perhaps, just perhaps, they still might get home by midnight, before her mother finished her work clearing up at the party of one of her employers. Emma wondered how the proctors knew about the plans for the ball. Everyone had been sworn to secrecy.

Another hour passed, during which time Emma heard Matron locking and unlocking cell doors. She wasn't aware that the vice chancellor had arrived. She didn't know a second round of questioning was under way. Only the men sitting in the 'courtroom' knew that the committal documentation – the formal papers used to authorise the imprisonment of women in the Spinning House – had already been completed, despite the fact that none of them had, as yet, stood trial.

Louisa Locker, Emma's half-sister, was first to be interrogated. Matron returned the pale-faced girl to the room she had been questioned in earlier. There, Louisa came face to face with the vice chancellor. The deep scarlet of his academic gown underscored the fearful severity of the situation. There he sat, surrounded by the four proctors who had questioned her earlier. The room was under his command. Louisa feared she might faint as a fuzziness swam into her body.

'Does your sister often take you out in the evening?' the vice chancellor asked.

'Yes. Yes, she does,' she told him. 'Sometimes we go to the post office,' she added, trying to be as helpful as she could.

'Is your sister often out at night?' he pressed.

'Never, no. Never after dark, Sir,' Louisa emphasised.

'Well then, go straight home. But remember, if I ever see you out again at night, I will lock you up. Oh, and tell your mother your sister will be detained here a little longer.'

Unknown to Emma, her fate had been sealed the moment Blore's paper knife glided through the top fold of the envelope enclosing the incriminating letter. Emma Kemp was, it implied, the ringleader of the illicit event. She should receive the greatest punishment. But before then, the vice chancellor had a further five young women to punish.

They were summoned one by one. Twenty-year-old Sarah Ebbon, 18-year-old Charlotte Fuller and 19-year-old Emma Coxall were each given a three-day sentence. Rosetta Aves, 17, was 'admonished and discharged'. Harriet Bell, 22 years old, tainted with uncertainty about a previous arrest, received a seven-day sentence.

Finally, Emma Kemp faced the vice chancellor. She had no idea she already stood implicated as the ringleader; no idea that her sister was already almost home; no idea her committal paperwork had been completed. All she knew was that she was innocent.

'What kind of party were you were going to?' asked the vice chancellor.

'A very respectable one, Sir, or I should not have joined it,' she replied.

'What time were you to return?'

'Half-past eleven or twelve.' Emma faced the questioning in the belief she would soon be released, with the misunderstanding explained away.

'Did you know the gentleman in the omnibus who invited you to the party?'

'Yes,' Emma said.

'How did you come to join the party?'

'I thought it a very respectable one.'

Emma explained she had made enquiries as to the propriety of the plans. All had seemed in order. Still, she had no suspicion of what was in store for her.

'Why did you take your sister?'

'The invitation was for two, so I took her.'

'Did you know if breakfast was ordered at the inn?'

The suggestion that breakfast had been ordered was later strongly denied in court. But the idea, invented by the letter writer, had strengthened the mountain of imagined evidence against Emma.

'We were coming home by twelve,' Emma reminded the vice chancellor.

Believing that the truth would prevail, she entreated the men before her to apply for character references from the ladies she worked for.

Her request was met with silence.

'I think none of these gentlemen know me,' she implored. Again, no words were uttered.

'Can I speak to my sister?' she begged.

'Your sister has been sent home,' the vice chancellor informed her, and without further questioning, he told her, 'I sentence you to fourteen days' imprisonment for being a loose and disorderly woman and being found in the company of members of the university.'

The hearing was over. No character witnesses were sought. Emma was rendered speechless as Matron steered her back to the cell she had vacated barely fifteen minutes before.

The vice chancellor and his men might have congratulated them-selves on such leniency if they had consulted the Committal Book dated 1823–49. The scratchy ledgers record that in 1824, Martha Jackson and Ann Harvey were sentenced to six weeks for being found at a dance at Howe House with gownsmen. But back in her cell, the only thought gnawing away inside Emma's head, as she tried to find some warmth in the bitterly cold cell, was how would she ever face her mother again?

Meanwhile, her frightened sister had fled back across Parker's Piece with the same fear of facing her mother. Slipping through the back door of the unlit house, she crumpled into a heap of dark misery to wait for her mother's return. Three long dark hours stretched out before her as she crouched like a wounded animal in the darkness of the family home, muddling together the words that would greet her worn-out mother.

8

RESPECTABILITY
AND RUIN

It was midnight when Mrs Locker crept through the back door of her home in Dover Street. Her weary hands fumbled as she undid the ribbons and buttons fastening her hat and coat. She longed for the comfort of her bed.

Louisa suddenly appeared at her side. The thin darkness disguised Louisa's blotched and swollen face, but her voice betrayed that all was far from well. It only took minutes for Louisa to blurt out the shameful words she had been rehearsing for hours and for the family's lives to change for ever. Mrs Locker knew ruin faced them all. Who would employ women tainted by the Spinning House?

Mother and daughter fell into bed holding each other tight. But every hour she was awake, and the few minutes she wasn't, Mrs Locker churned over what to do. She wrestled with ideas to prevent their disgrace. At some point, in the early hours of Tuesday, 31 January, an idea instilled itself. She was a respectable woman. Her daughter had made a silly mistake. It was simple. She would go to the vice chancellor that morning and plead for Emma's release.

The sun had barely risen as Mrs Locker retied and buttoned the hat and coat she'd tossed aside a few hours before. Under her arm was a precious parcel containing a clean dress, warm shawl and fresh ale. She crossed the road from Barnwell and onto Parker's Piece.

Parker's Piece was the only large area of open ground owned by the town. Once edging the open fields tended by the monks from Barnwell Abbey, it now acted as an invisible boundary between the rich and poor. A light frost covered the short spikes of grass covering the Piece as Mrs Locker hurried along, her head looking firmly down.

As she emerged into Regent Street, the noise of the town waking up confronted her. It was a relief. The grinding sound of cartwheels and horses' hooves helped muffle the sound of her repeated ringing and hammering on the doors of the Spinning House. But inside, in the quiet of the stone walls, no one came to her aid.

In desperation, Mrs Locker was forced to shout. 'I want to see the vice chancellor!' she cried. But still no one came.

Eventually, she heard a bolt being drawn back and the prison door creaked open a fraction. Matron peered through the narrow gap to deliver a blunt message. 'You can't see anyone,' she announced, closing the door in the mother's distraught face.

Thinking fast, Mrs Locker wedged her foot in the door before Matron could close it. 'I demand to see the proctors,' she insisted.

There was a short struggle, which Matron won as she kicked the irritating woman's foot away, firmly banging the prison doors in her face.

Anguish enveloped the mother. What could she do now? She decided to hide in the shadow of a nearby doorway in the hope that a senior member of the university might appear.

The waiting paid off. After half an hour, she spotted the vice chancellor striding towards the prison. Darting out in front of him, she pleaded, 'I must speak with you, Sir!' He took no notice of her as he swept through the Spinning House entrance, cautiously monitored by a vigilant Matron.

Refusing to give up, she again tried hammering on the hard oak of the Spinning House gates. 'Let me in or I shall die!' she screamed.

Eventually, the door opened, and this time, under instruction from the vice chancellor, Matron ushered Mrs Locker inside. 'You can have fifteen minutes with the prisoner.'

Prisoner! In that moment her stomach received an invisible blow. Her child was a prisoner. How could this be?

'Follow me,' Matron commanded.

Mrs Locker forced deep breaths into her tightening chest as she heard the jangling sound of keys unlocking a first door, then, as the two women crossed the same cold, stone inner courtyard of the prison hall, where almost fourteen hours earlier Emma and Louisa had stood huddled together, a second door was unlocked. This opened into a small room, the same whitewashed room her two daughters had been interrogated in the previous evening. There, she was temporarily reunited, under the keen eye of Matron, with her child.

She was shocked. Emma, no longer in her party clothes, wore the prison uniform: a coarse checked dress of inferior clothing, the kind worn by someone of a much lower class – a humiliating experience for both mother and daughter.

'I've brought a clean dress, a shawl and some ale.' Mrs Locker offered up the lovingly wrapped bundle.

'I can't allow them,' Matron replied.

'But the dress …'

Mrs Locker was curtly cut off by Matron. 'It's against prison regulations!' she snapped.

But touching each other was not against the rules. Tears and sobs flowed as the pair clung to each other in sorrow and grief. But such a noisy display of emotion proved too much for Matron.

'If you can't control yourselves and keep quiet, I shall return the prisoner to her cell,' she threatened.

Through their tears, the mother and daughter conversed. Feelings of remorse from Emma, a promise to get her out from her mother. But all too soon, Mrs Locker was forced to say goodbye.

'I'll try,' she called as Matron led Emma back to the cells, while the under matron returned Mrs Locker to the blur of the outside world. Nothing mattered to her now except proving Emma's innocence and gaining her release.

Emma noticed a softening in Matron after her mother's visit. Perhaps it was obvious that Mrs Locker was a caring and respectable woman. Evidence indicates that she was the only one of the mothers of the five newly incarcerated girls to fight for her daughter's release.

Emboldened by Matron's mellowing and with hours of monotony facing her, Emma braved a request. 'Could I have something to do to pass the time? Perhaps some plain needlework, some mending or I could make something?'

The under matron returned with some needlework, but Emma struggled with her stitches. Her fingers were so cold it was almost impossible to hold the needle for any length of time. The new heating system, so recently installed due to the national outcry following the death of Elizabeth Howe, was not up to the job after all. Luckily, the new matron employed to replace the cruel and chaotic keeper, Mr Wilson, was up to the job. Even if the building still lacked warmth, the inmates didn't have to pay for their food or be dragged about by their hair if they raised their voices to protest.

Later that afternoon, the prison surgeon, Mr Fawcett, arrived for his daily rounds. One by one, the new girls were called into a room to be questioned. Finally, it was Emma's turn.

'Name? Address?' he asked.

'Emma Kemp. Dover Street. I work for the wife of your partner, Mr Hough,' she confidently told him. She stitched for many respected families in the town.

'You are well?' he asked. 'Do you take any medicines?'

These first questions were routine enough.

'Are you suffering from disease?'

'What do you mean, Sir?' Emma asked. 'I am well. I am not suffering …'

She suddenly paused. For the first time since her arrest her body felt like it was on fire as the significance of the grotesque question dawned on her. She wanted to shout out, 'How dare you!' but instead she heard herself say, 'No, Sir. I am not.' Her humiliation, standing in front of this important man wearing the uniform of a servant, was now complete.

Women forced into the Spinning House were not compulsorily examined. Although, under Mr Oakes, medical officer between 1828 and 1841, it had been a place where diseased women were able to seek treatment. Unfortunately, his record book does not survive, but treatment was free and could take between two to three weeks. Under Mr Oakes, roughly 5 per cent of the girls arrested received treatment for venereal disease. Under Mr Fawcett, only 1 per cent of those arrested were suffering from the disease, but with the use of euphemistic words such as 'unwell' or 'ill', it is impossible to paint a full picture of the health of all the women arrested by the proctors. However, this evidence suggests that it wasn't a significant problem.

Emma was arrested in 1860, four years before the Contagious Diseases Act made it perfectly legal to force an invasive medical examination on women suspected of being prostitutes. One cannot underestimate the indignity of the question being asked of an innocent young woman such as Emma Kemp.

As the daily prison routine began for Emma – bread for breakfast and what was called 'soup', consisting of dripping and potatoes, for dinner, then supper, a kind of gruel – outside, Mrs Locker was finding inner reserves of strength in her battle to secure her daughter's release and restore the family's untarnished name.

Mr Hough, the surgeon for whom Mrs Locker and Emma both worked, promised to put in a good word with the vice chancellor, but

Mrs Locker knew a plea to her most influential employer, Dr Pulling, Master of Corpus Christi College, was her best chance.

On Saturday, 4 February, she went to Corpus Christi College, entering, as usual, through the servants' gate in a back street. From there to the Master's Lodge and to the master's study. Dr Pulling did indeed hold this hard-working honest woman in high esteem. Her plea for help landed on sympathetic ears. He agreed to write a note to the vice chancellor vouching for the family's respectability.

With the freshly blotted and sealed letter in her grateful, warmly gloved hands, Mrs Locker set off through streets bustling with activity to another Master's Lodge. This time Magdalene College. On the way, she rehearsed the words she would say to the vice chancellor.

Dodging anyone she knew, she neared Bridge Street, the industrial heart of Cambridge where the narrow yards and courts buzzed with noisy activity. The pungent aroma of industry filled her nostrils. Wharves and warehouses lined the riverbank. Horses and carts were laden with cargos of corn and coal. Bargemen, dressed in their distinctive crimson and blue long-sleeved waistcoats with buttons made of glass, shouted to each other as they loaded and unloaded consignments. The smells from Finches Iron Foundry, a mustard and vinegar factory and Ekin's Brewery filled the air as she crossed the river towards Magdalene College, the only college sitting north of the river. As she walked through the ancient gates of Magdalene College, which had originally been a Benedictine monastery, she crossed the same square of tranquil green that proctors Blore and Woollaston had traversed days before, clutching the letter damming her daughter.

She took a deep breath. She knocked on the door of another Master's Lodge. The Honourable Reverend Latimer Neville, 6th Baron Braybrooke, wasn't surprised to see her. 'I've made enquiries about you and your daughter,' he told her. 'And received excellent characters.'

'Thank you, Sir.' Mrs Locker's knees bobbed in a small curtsy. 'Sir, I've a letter.' She put the prized possession in her hand onto his desk, unsure if she should hand it directly to him.

He picked it up to digest its contents while the nervous mother forced herself to stay silent. The note confirmed the vice chancellor's enquiries about Emma Kemp and Mrs Locker.

'I will write a note for her immediate release,' he announced. 'Take it to the Spinning House and she will be able to accompany you home.'

The wave of relief that swept through Mrs Locker almost overwhelmed her, but her ability to react quickly in a crisis had not forsaken her.

Mindful of the shame of Emma being spotted leaving the Spinning House, she asked the vice chancellor, 'Sorry Sir, could she be discharged under the cover of darkness and sent home in a fly? Mr Hough the surgeon has said he will pay the expense.'

It was agreed, and later that Saturday evening, Emma returned home, albeit still wearing the clothes providing a cruel reminder of the innocent excitement of five nights ago.

But the cover of darkness and a fly did not guarantee concealment. As news of the wrongful arrest of seven innocent young women reached the editors of several London newspapers, smouldering hostilities between town and gown flared up once again. Emma Kemp's name, far from being concealed, was splashed on the pages of newspapers up and down the country. Her ordeal was far from over.

9

THE LAW OF THE LAND VS THE VICE CHANCELLOR

he Hoop Hotel, on the corner of Bridge Street, where the young poet William Wordsworth had famously alighted in 1787, possessed two superior reception rooms, making it a favourite place to hold political meetings. On the evening of 16 February 1860, the stairs of the old coaching inn creaked under the weight of the steps of free-thinking businessmen who'd been specially selected to attend a secret summit being held in one of the hotel's freshly decorated reception rooms.

Seventeen eventful days had passed since the arrest of Emma Kemp and her fellow partygoers. It wasn't long before news of the clandestine ball had spread as far as the capital. The *Daily Telegraph* published an article attacking 'The Proctorial System at Cambridge'. Its editor, Mr Thornton Leigh Hunt, an ardent Liberal reformer, had had a tip-off and delighted in telling the story of the 'University men's spree'. 'Is this an example of the liberty of the English subject?' the article demanded to know. Readers responded with letters about 'pig-headed conduct' at Cambridge.

In Cambridge, as elsewhere, the tide against the landowning classes was turning. That year, the Cambridge Liberal and Conservative Parties had won equal representation in the municipal elections, which was quite a win, given that it was claimed that 200 Liberal sympathisers failed to vote for fear of university influence preventing them from earning a living.

Long gone were the days when a Whig investigation, carried out in Cambridge in 1833, exposed the inconvenient fact that, under the influence of Mayor Mortlock's family, £1,300 of rate payers' money had been spent on celebratory dinners attended by councillors and those whose votes they courted, with only £450 spent on the good of the town.

Since then, five newly constituted wards had been established, reflecting the growth in population – five seats the Liberal Party was determined to win.

The storm still raged about the arrest and imprisonment of Emma Kemp and the other six young women forced inside the Spinning House prison. On the streets of Cambridge, brawls were breaking out as rescue attempts on women spotted in the clutches of the proctors increased.

One scuffle played into the welcome hands of a small band of professionally educated, liberal-minded men. Some of these had been educated at Cambridge, but all knew, after the success of the memorial fought by councillors following the death of Elizabeth Howe, that the assumed centuries-old privileges of the university could be dismantled – and it was these men who were climbing the stairs of the recently renovated Hoop Hotel, invigorated by a legal challenge to a recent skirmish on the town's streets.

A few days before, a young apprentice girl had been hounded by a proctor and his Bulldogs as she walked home from the shop where she worked.

'What's your name?' the proctor demanded as his men encircled her.

Fear turned the girl into a muddle of panic. Speech became impossible.

'Where are you going?' A second question, harsher than the first, was fired at her.

It hit her senses, causing a wave of dizziness.

'Where do you live?' The loud voice, pounding on.

'Leave her alone!' someone cried out. 'Can't you see how frightened she is?'

'I know her – she is an apprentice girl!' another shouted.

'Will you vouch for her character?' the proctor asked.

'I do, Sir.'

As the proctor and his men moved on, the shaken girl fled home to her father, who was outraged at the insult to the character of his daughter. Straight away, he went out to find the proctor. He demanded a written apology for the mistake. The proctor refused but yielded with an expression of regret.

Regret, however, was not enough to right the wrong. The next day, the girl's father went to see his solicitor. There, he issued instructions to demand a letter of apology from the proctor.

It took several days for a reluctant apology to arrive via the proctor's solicitor. This closed the matter for the family, but the seed of an idea had been planted, one that took root in the mind of the solicitor. That lawman was one of the men rushing up the staircase of the Hoop Hotel to attend the secret meeting being held that February evening, carrying with him a perfectly incubated plan that he was itching to reveal.

Secrecy about the gathering prevented the reporter from the *Cambridge Independent* newspaper disclosing the names of the individuals attending the meeting on that early spring evening. Later, he approvingly styled them the 'Committee of Gentlemen Opposed to Proctorial Powers'. We can, however, be sure of the names of two of the influential gentlemen who climbed the carpeted staircase of the Hoop Hotel. One was Mr William Cockerell who, at 34, was already an experienced solicitor known for his persuasive eloquence. His father had been a college servant – one resenting the obsequious deference he must daily submit to. He did all he could to make certain his son would not follow in his own footsteps.

William Cockerell, a bright and determined boy, didn't follow in his father's footsteps. He was articled to Charles Henry Cooper, who had fought hard at the inquest into the death of Elizabeth Howe to end the tyranny of the proctors.

Like Cooper, Cockerell was determined to redress the balance of power in Cambridge. He became the highly respected Liberal representative for Barnwell, where he recognised a growing population of over 9,000 working men and women needed more than a vicar, two curates and a scripture reader to help them rise above the economic uncertainty damning their daily lives. He helped set up the Barnwell Reform Association for the promotion of civil and religious liberty.

When running in the municipal elections, he stated 'he cared not one iota' what the university and its supporters thought of him. He was a long-standing member of the Liberal Party and for many years was Secretary of the Liberal Association. He eagerly sprang up the softly furnished stairs of the Hoop Hotel.

The second influential gentleman attending the secret meeting was Mr Thompson Cooper, the 23-year-old son of the now ailing Charles Henry Cooper. He was his father's son, through and through. Trained as a solicitor and being articled to his father, he was also sub-editor of the *Daily Telegraph*, and, like his father, he was already an antiquarian of some repute – he'd gained veneration for ably helping his father to complete further volumes of the famed *Annals of Cambridge*. Here was an educated and highly respected man who, like Cockerell, wasn't cowed by the university. A man who, like his father, suspected legal scrutiny of the ancient charter authorising the detention of women 'suspected of evil' would prove it defective.

One by one that evening, men who were determined to see the end of proctorial authority and the Spinning House gathered in the large meeting room of the hotel. Secrecy about the meeting ensured that those present could speak without fear of reprisal from factions supportive of the university.

The evening started, and ended, with a clear purpose. It was about the townspeople and its women; their right to justice and liberty – the same as every other woman in the land. 'Gentlemen, we must right wrongs,' Cockerell began. 'Had the omnibus contained two townsmen instead of two townsmen, the apprehension and detention of the girls by the proctors would have been illegal. If a townsman is caught by the proctor in the embrace of a frail fair one, does he interfere? No, he does not. He is there only to protect the weakness of his own.'

Cries of 'Hear, hear!' rang out.

'The powers of the university subvert the liberty of the subject!' someone shouted.

'Hear, hear!'

'They are repugnant to the feelings of the inhabitants of this town!' cried out another.

'Hear, hear!'

Complaints, frustrations and cheers continued until the eloquent voice of Mr William Cockerell stilled them. 'Fourteen years ago, following the death of Elizabeth Howe, the coroner, Charles Henry Cooper, advised her parents they could challenge the authority of the proctor in arresting their daughter.'

An assenting murmur was heard in the room. It was true there was some uncertainty that the centuries-old privilege would not stand modern-day legal scrutiny. Cockerell paused for a moment. He wanted his next words to fully register in the ears and minds of every man present.

'Recently, a father received a written apology from a proctor for wrongly harassing his daughter. I advised the parents they could sue for damages.' Cockerell hinted at the plan he was poised to unveil. 'Wishing to protect their daughter from the distress of a court hearing, the parents decided against further legal action.' Courage and money were needed before launching a challenge against the university.

'But,' he cried out, as he reached the crescendo of his moment in the spotlight, 'I am happy to offer a small sum to assist with legal action against the university. Perhaps others will join me?'

A short silence followed, when all that could be heard was the flicker of flames jumping and crackling as they licked at the logs in the large, ornate fireplace at one end of the room. It was time to test the ancient laws of the university against the common law of the land.

The excitement at the idea of collective action to thwart further harassment of wives, daughters and female servants energised the room. Cheers burst out as fast as hands were raised to pledge support. Then and there, a fund was founded to guarantee financial support to anyone instigating legal proceedings against the university for wrongful arrest.

That evening, before the men left the warmth of the Hoop Hotel, two important resolutions had been passed and were later published in the local newspapers:

It is the opinion of this meeting that the powers exercised by the Proctors and the Vice Chancellor in the apprehension and imprisonment of females are opposed to the spirit of the English constitution, subversive of the liberty of the subject, repugnant to the feelings of the inhabitants of this town and wholly inoperative as affecting the objects which they profess to accomplish.

That with the view of effecting an alteration of the system, a subscription be forthwith opened for raising funds to take the necessary steps to carry out that object.

Speculation about the fund spread rapidly. Rumour had it that over £100 had been committed, with more anticipated.

News of the fund infuriated senior members of the university and its supporters. Three hundred and sixty men signed a petition to preserve 'Proctorial Jurisdiction'. On close inspection, it transpired that 260 of those were either members of the university, its servants or college tradesmen. Only 100 signatories were from people unconnected to the university.

The townspeople retaliated. Posters and pamphlets tumbled off printing presses. The petition was flawed. Many town dignitaries, including the mayor, four borough justices, eight aldermen, twenty-two councillors, the town clerk, the clerk to the magistrates, as well as the 12,000 male inhabitants of the town, had not been invited to sign the university's document. It was hardly a barometer of the true feelings in the town.

Letters supporting the university and deriding the fund appeared in the *Cambridge Chronicle*. 'It is a scheme dreamt up by two radical attorneys planning to reap the rewards of compensation,' scoffed one correspondent.

'At least four or five brewers and publicans were present,' mocked another. Landowners always trumped trade in the minds of the upper classes.

'Any women foolish and misguided enough to challenge the Vice Chancellor will be disappointed,' another warned.

A great number of scathing remarks derided the fact that the names of those supporting the fund had not been published, nor the leaders of the meeting named. Yet, for such a fund to succeed, secrecy was essential. There was a price to pay for upsetting the university, but the seven innocent young women, whose secret plans had been so cruelly disclosed, had everything to gain – and gain it they would – if they could.

A few days after the meeting at the Hoop Hotel, Emma Kemp, branded by the vice chancellor as the ringleader of the ill-fated 'ball spree', made her way to Fitzwilliam Street to knock on the door of Mr William Cockerell. He was delighted to see her. He was impatient to test the legitimacy of the despised laws oppressing the women in the town.

With tears rolling down her cheeks, Emma told Cockerell of her desperate plight. With her character tarnished by her arrest, work had dried up. No longer could the respectable ladies of Cambridge risk their own ruin by having any association with her.

'But you were released once your character was known!' Sympathy, anger and frustration boiled up inside him as the two talked over the fateful events of the night of 30 January. 'It's a case of wrongful arrest,' Cockerell said. 'It must be fought in a court of law.'

Emma agreed to allow him to petition the vice chancellor for wrongful arrest and imprisonment, assuming the matter would be tried in Cambridge and Emma's good character quietly restored once the facts were known. But as the paperwork for *Kemp vs Neville* was begun, news arrived that Harriet Bell and Sarah Ebbon had visited Thompson Cooper, residing in Jesus Lane with his father, Charles. They too planned to sue the vice chancellor.

Then came the news that another woman had been snatched off the streets and marched into the Spinning House; a woman whose husband sought revenge.

On the evening of 28 March, 30-year-old Mrs Grindle Cattaway, a laundress, was returning some linen to a customer in Trinity Street when she bumped into two fellow laundresses, Harriet Betson and Miss Brockwell, in St Andrew's Street. The women stopped for a chat. Within minutes, the trio were spotted by the proctor and his Bulldogs. Two of the women were alarmed as they had been arrested and imprisoned in the Spinning House before – evidence enough, to the proctors, that they were 'streetwalkers'. The proctor decided the third older, unknown woman in their company must be a brothel keeper. All three were marched to the Spinning House.

'I won't go in!' Mrs Cattaway shouted as they neared the prison doors. 'I've done nothing wrong!' she yelled out as she tried to break free. 'I'm a married woman.'

A small crowd of onlookers gathered to witness the spectacle. Shaking herself free of her captors, Mrs Cattaway ran off. Would she get away, the crowd wondered?

She didn't. Within 30 yards, she felt the heavy hands of the Bulldogs grasping her shoulders. Under their firm hold, she was dragged to the Spinning House and shoved through its doors.

Escape was impossible. Fuming with anger, she was forced to wait in a small, cold cobbled courtyard before being taken to a small whitewashed room to be formally interviewed by the arresting proctor, Mr Barnard Smith.

'What have you to say for yourself?' Barnard Smith asked.

'It is a very cruel thing to be taken,' she curtly announced. 'I work for respectable shops in the town.' Indignant at her arrest, she refused to cower before the man who held her economic prosperity in his hands. 'This arrest will injure my character,' she scolded.

'Are you a married woman?' Barnard Smith asked.

'I am.'

'Then why were you talking to two prostitutes?'

'I did not consider them prostitutes as I know they work for a living as laundresses,' she said.

'You must see how wrong it is to walk the streets with prostitutes at night,' the proctor chided her.

'I did not know they were prostitutes,' she repeated.

A moment of silence passed while Barnard Smith weighed up both the evidence and, more importantly, the morality of the accused. Then, with a dismissive wave, he told her, 'I will detain you here no longer.'

But her humiliation was not at an end. As she squeezed through the partly open prison doors, praying no one would see her, a sea of peering faces moved in her direction. The crowd, who had been busy speculating her fate, still lingered outside the prison gates. Her reputation was in tatters.

Four months later, Barnard Smith would face Mrs Cattaway again. Not in Cambridge but in the Court of Common Pleas at Westminster Hall. The vice chancellor, alarmed that the court cases stacking up against the university would lead to violent reprisals, negotiated an out-of-town venue for the legal wranglings. *Mr Cattaway and Wife vs Smith*; *Kemp vs Neville*; *Ebbon vs Neville* and *Bell vs Neville* would be heard by the Lord Chief Justice, defended by top barristers and judged by a London jury. The stakes had risen. So, too, had the legal costs.

10

THE COURT OF COMMON PLEAS, WESTMINSTER HALL

I t was a fine summer's morning when Emma Kemp gathered up her skirts to step onto the crowded platform at Bishopsgate Station in London. She was accompanied by her mother, half-sister Louisa and the other women litigating against Cambridge University.

Strict laws, made by the university, which was always fearful of the morals of day trippers making their way to Cambridge, limited Sunday train services to early morning or late afternoon. Thus, it had been agreed that Emma Kemp, Mrs Cattaway, Harriet Bell, Sarah Ebbon and their witnesses would depart for London on Saturday, 16 June, two days before the date of the trials.

It was a big moment in the history of town and gown relations – a crucial time for their lawyers, too. This was going to be a bitterly fought battle. Reputations were at stake. Many were eager to witness the legal battle between two top barristers, which would be staged in the majestic surroundings of Westminster Hall.

Would Emma Kemp clear her name? If she did, she was set to recover damages of £500, which would secure the family a comfortable future without elevating them too far beyond their station. It had been four months since four wrongly arrested women had decided to press charges against the university. But there was no certainty as to which party would prevail.

That weekend, London was whirring with excitement for another reason. The distant rumble of drums was heard as the party from Cambridge stepped off the train to make their way to lodgings nearby. Around them, 320 men of the Civil Service Rifles were also stepping off trains ready to march to Regent's Park for the dress rehearsal of Queen Victoria's military review, due to be held the following Saturday.

'Can we watch?' cried an excited Louisa.

'We're not here for that,' her mother scolded.

'I'll escort her and my wife,' volunteered a gallant Mr Cattaway.

Mrs Locker was unsure. All she could think about was the very serious reason the group were in London. She looked at their solicitor for advice.

'It might be soothing,' he suggested.

Correspondents to the *Cambridge Chronicle* would later ridicule the two days the group spent in London, mocking that the fund had paid for a sightseeing holiday. But Louisa and Mrs Cattaway were eager sightseers and were in for a treat. More regiments began to arrive. Soon Regent's Park swelled with 2,500 volunteers and the trio got caught up in the cheering crowds flocking to catch a sight of the regiments practising wheeling right, then left, under the loud orders of their commanders.

In the gentle morning sunshine of Monday, 18 June 1860, the walls of the new Palace of Westminster almost shimmered as Emma Kemp, accompanied by Mr Cockerell, her mother and half-sister Louisa, lifted their straw-bonneted heads to peer up at the grand building as they walked under the grand arched entrance of Westminster Hall.

They took in the sights, sounds and smells around them – the aroma of the River Thames was never at its best on warm, sunny days. Walking beside them, a cheerful Cockerell was quietly optimistic about the day ahead – and it was reassuring for the women to have such a man by their side, and on their side.

It was nearly nine o'clock, an hour before the Lord Chief Justice, Judge William Erle, was due to arrive. Demand for the limited number of seats inside the courtroom was high. In the busy throng, no one took much notice of the attractive brown-haired young woman also searching for a seat. Emma's case was third on the list that day, allowing her the luxury of time to observe the workings of a court. *Crosse vs Martin* was first on the list, followed by *Mr Cattaway and Wife vs The Reverend Barnard Smith* – the warm-up for *Kemp vs Neville* – the highlight of the day.

'Here, sit in those seats.' Cockerell came to the rescue of Mrs Locker and her daughters. He indicated three seats to the rear of the court. 'The judge sits on that raised platform.' A kind Cockerill pointed to the focal point of the room, a dais lavishly hung with rich swathes of scarlet cloth. In the well of the court, four long, curved, high-backed wooden benches creaked minute by minute as numerous wigged and gowned men took their seats.

'They are the attorneys, king's sergeants and counsel,' Cockerell explained. 'I'll sit there when your case is called.' He then pointed to a large box to their right. 'That's where the jury sit.'

Opposite was another box, big enough only for a single person, and that was where each member of the family would take it in turns to stand when the time came; all three were anxious at the thought.

The Lord Chancellor's courtroom was adorned with a glass dome in the ceiling, encircled by equally splendid skylights. The wooden seating below had taken on a soft sheen as sunlight bathed the room. It seemed odd to Emma that the world had not come to a complete standstill, such was her anxiety about how the day would unfold. As the temperature and tensions climbed that day, the place would become suffocatingly hot.

In the distance, a bell signalled that ten o'clock had arrived. All rose to acknowledge the entrance of the Lord Chief Justice in his ermine-trimmed scarlet robes, his horsehair wig matching the grey of his sideburns. As the day wore on, his naturally ruddy complexion would show the rising heat of the room.

The first task was to hear *Crosse vs Martin*, a case to recover costs after the promise of funds for the construction of a railway line between Newport and Cowes. It was a voluminous case. The sound of the quarter bell inside the new Bell Tower of the Palace of Westminster tracked each long hour as the finer details of the case were hammered out. One o'clock was reached. The court broke for lunch. *Crosse vs Martin* resumed at two o'clock.

Emma fretted as the time slipped by. In her mind, she was stitching together each section of the day, each piece moving her closer to her own ordeal. Cockerell tried to reassure her. 'It takes time,' he said, a deep breath to relieving the tension building up in his own shoulders.

As time dragged, those sitting in the public seats craved fresh, cool air and wandered in and out of the cramped room.

It was 3.30 in the afternoon when *Mr Cattaway and Wife vs The Reverend Barnard Smith* was finally called. It was rather a novel moment to witness a washerwoman litigate against a university proctor. Seats refilled and six special jurors, all London merchants, together with six common jurors were sworn in. Damages for Mrs Cattaway for false arrest were set at £500 – the same as those set for Emma Kemp.

The university had engaged Mr O'Malley QC; Thompson Cooper had engaged Edwin James QC. James was a man lacking in natural good looks, which had hampered his first ambition to become an actor so he had turned to the law as being the next best thing. He had the look and determination of a prize fighter, winning fame for his successful pleading in cases for seduction, breach of promise of marriage, assault and false imprisonment. He was notable for his successes defending cases involving the reputations of actresses. As Liberal MP for Marylebone, he was well known for his 'radical sympathies'.

Emma turned her professional dressmaking eyes on the legal men in the courtroom. The QCs, she noticed, wore black silk gowns, white shirts, white collar bands and bristly wigs. The junior men wore gowns of a coarser black cloth. She watched closely as James, who, Emma thought, had a slight disregard for the tailoring of his legal garb, rose with measured precision. He wanted to capture the gaze of every eye in the room. Slowly, he pivoted his body to face his most important audience, the twelve men settled in the jury box.

'This is a case deserving serious consideration,' he began, his voice reaching every ear of the assembled crowd. 'Mrs Grindle Cattaway is the wife of a man who, though in humble circumstances, is a highly respectable employee of the Eastern Counties Railway Company. The question here is simply to establish if the accused did what she has been accused of.' He paused for dramatic effect and to fill his lungs with the stale air coming off the sweltering bodies packed into the room. 'I will prove that it was under the Reverend Barnard Smith's orders that this innocent woman was arrested and temporarily imprisoned, that her cruel entry and exit from the Spinning House Prison was witnessed by a number of people, stamping her with the stigma of being a woman of the town.'

His confident air impressed Emma, even if his tailoring didn't. The 48-year-old QC had a commanding manner, proudly jutting his chin out as he spoke. His long sideburns lengthened the scrupulous look of his face. Some of her worries began to fade. Here was certainly a fighting man.

James mocked the archaic laws of Cambridge University that 'interfered with the liberty of the subject'. The proctors, he said, claimed the right to go up to any woman in the town and say, 'I suspect you of being improper' and order them off to the Spinning House where, without evidence on oath, the vice chancellor sentenced the unhappy women to a fortnight, a month, or more.

Laugher at the absurdity of the proctors' powers in the modern age rippled round the room as James explained how the plaintiff had been speaking with two women she knew, when 'the Bulldogs – a good name for this species of semi-constables as their doings caused constant scenes of violence in the town, hounded her off the street and into the Spinning House'. Although she had only been inside the prison for half an hour, this confinement had seriously affected her character. 'Even up to this time,' he declared, 'the stigma of her association with that prison remained with her, affecting her opportunities for work.'

This was the same situation Emma Kemp faced as her respectable work as a dressmaker had dried up since her arrest. James continued that Mrs Cattaway 'had done nothing wrong. Nothing that could give offence to any human being, or in any way excuse the treatment she had received by order of the defendant.' Nor had she broken the law of the land.

A wave of nerves ran through Emma when she spotted Mrs Cattaway being escorted to the witness stand. Emma watched as the neatly dressed woman, her hair parted beneath her flaring bonnet, gathered up her skirts in readiness to ascend the handful of steps into the witness box. Did everyone hear each rustling step as Mrs Cattaway climbed into the stand? Emma did. She was alert to every move, every sound, as she absorbed every moment; it wasn't calming her nerves.

'I am Mrs Cattaway. I am the wife of a fireman on the Eastern Counties Railway. He works on the Hitchin Line,' her voice rang out. Taking her cue from James, Mrs Cattaway relayed every detail of her cruel arrest. When she had finished, O'Malley, the university's QC, moved into position for the cross-examination. O'Malley's gown was a perfect fit, Emma observed, but his bearing in the room seemed insignificant compared to James's.

O'Malley was a diligent legal man, but his delivery was slow and uninteresting. However, what he lacked in flair was bolstered by the sheaf of papers by his side. He had been a busy man and had been ruthlessly snooping around in Barnwell. He had tittle-tattle-filled pages of sworn statements. He was poised to deliver a blow to the prize-fighting tactics of James.

'Mrs Cattaway,' he announced, 'lives in Barnwell, a notorious part of Cambridge, where young single females lodge in her house.'

'I do not.' An indignant Mrs Cattaway was quick to correct the QC. 'I live in Broad Street. It is not in the area called Barnwell. I have lodgers in my house, but I never have more than one unmarried woman at a time. A girl named Durrant lodged with me once.' She volunteered the unasked information anticipating a backlash as the girl had recently resorted to prostitution. 'She was not a common girl then. She made her living by washing and mangling. I swear that I never had anything improper going on in my house.'

'Why were you out on the streets on the evening of 28 March?' O'Malley asked.

'I don't always know the dates when the university term begins or ends,' protested Mrs Cattaway. 'If I did, I certainly wouldn't have gone out the same night the proctor and his men were walking the streets.'

Amused tittering filled the courtroom. The trial was proving an entertaining day out for some. But such frivolity, together with the almost intolerable heat inside the room, was turning O'Malley into a very uncomfortable man.

'You launder dirty linen for immoral women,' he spat the accusation at her.

Mrs Cattaway was stunned. Emma Kemp felt the body blow too. She had been warned people had been snooping around Barnwell, rummaging for every piece of intimate tittle-tattle. Emma breathed a sigh of relief in the belief that such a search would prove fruitless in her case.

James caused much merriment in the room as he jumped up to defend the washerwoman. 'It is a shame,' he coolly observed, 'if such unfortunates are to be debarred from cleanliness.'

Emma relaxed. She liked this man. He was making a fool of the sneering O'Malley.

James next called three young women and three men, each swearing they'd witnessed the Bulldogs grab Mrs Cattaway and force her inside the Spinning House in the full view of the proctor.

'How do you earn a living?' O'Malley asked one of the women.

'I go out to needlework.'

'Is that sufficient to keep you?' he sneered.

'I earn 4s 6d making shirts for Mrs Easton in Cambridge Place,' she told him.

Emma heard the church bells outside striking five times. Her heart sank. Time was running out. A quarter of an hour later, the Lord Chief Justice made an announcement. 'I adjourn this case till ten o'clock tomorrow morning.' The party from Cambridge would need to prevail on the fund, set up on the night of the secret meeting at the Hoop Hotel, to pay for another night's stay in London.

The following morning, the public galleries filled again with eager spectators. It remained hard to tell which way the jury would go. Emma and her mother thought James had made O'Malley look foolish, but everything hinged on the examination of Barnard Smith. Emma watched as the proctor, his face and demeanour set solid, entered the witness box.

'For what reason did you arrest Mrs Cattaway?' James asked.

'I depend on my men for the character of the women I meet on my rounds,' he made clear. 'I did not intend taking her once I discovered she was a married woman, but my men mistook my instructions.'

'Why have the Bulldogs who recommended her arrest not been called as witnesses?' James wanted to know. 'Where is the evidence they had for advising her arrest?' Looking round the room, he declared, 'I see these special advisors are not called as witnesses.'

'It will be for the judge to decide if my client is answerable for the conduct of his men,' O'Malley flashed back. 'Mr Barnard Smith is a member of St Peter's College. We should be satisfied with his account. The rights claimed by the university might be distasteful to the lower classes of the town, but what justification has an advocate for bringing those matters before a jury?'

The pleadings at an end, the Lord Chief Justice addressed the jury. 'Mr Barnard Smith, it seems, did not mean to arrest Mrs Cattaway. Yet, he is liable for wrongful arrest under the circumstances,' he advised. 'Many anxious parents support the proctorial system at Cambridge, as long as it is carried out with due care and caution. Yet the defendant was carrying out his duty and could not be held responsible for the system under which he carried out that duty.' The jury retired to consider the conundrum.

During the fifteen minutes it took the dozen to deliberate, O'Malley asked the Lord Chief Justice if he could fix a new date for *Kemp vs Neville*. 'It is on the list for today,' he said, 'but it seems unlikely there will be sufficient time for it.'

It was anticipated the case would take two to three days and the leading counsel, Sir Fitzroy Kelly – rumoured to have been offered 150 guineas to represent the vice chancellor – was engaged in a case that was dragging on. A postponement of *Kemp vs Neville* was agreed. A date would be set for the next term.

The jury returned. 'Do you have a verdict?'

'We do.'

'Do you find the defendant, the Reverend Mr Barnard Smith, guilty or not guilty?'

'Guilty.'

Emma Kemp wanted to shout for joy. She couldn't believe the verdict.

'What figure do you set for damages?'

'We award Mrs Grindle Cattaway damages of £50.'

The question now was would *Kemp vs Neville* deliver a second resounding victory for the law of the land? And what use would the university authorities make of the interval before the next academic term to make certain every tiny scrap of evidence had been gathered?

11

SMEARS AND FEARS

There were no marching bands, soft blue skies or parades to distract Emma Kemp when she returned to London in November 1860. A cool easterly breeze ruffled the neat trimmings of her closely tied bonnet as she made her way, once again, to the Court of Common Pleas at Westminster Hall. It was the last day of November, a day that would be notable for a procession of Cambridge dons and Oxford men – out to obtain a day's amusement at their rivals' expense – all vying for seats in the already packed court. There was considerable apprehension in some quarters that the right of the university to arrest and imprison women might be ruled legally defective.

Eager spectators were cramming into every single seat. Latecomers climbed the staircase to squeeze along the viewing gallery elegantly edging the rim of the high-domed ceiling. The *Globe* newspaper later described the place as being 'crowded almost to suffocation'. Outside the courtroom, a swarm of people debated how the case might turn out. How would a dressmaker from Cambridge fare against the Vice Chancellor of Cambridge University? *Kemp vs Neville* was about to be begin.

Expectations for the plaintiff were high. The success of *Cattaway vs Smith* was still in the minds of the townspeople. It had caused ripples of panic within the university. The name of one don, put forward for election as proctor, had been hastily withdrawn when his reputation for rigid adherence to his duties was revealed. Arrests were down. Violence in the streets was up. A mob had even wrestled with a proctor taking a known prostitute to the Spinning House. Such was the anger in the town that unwanted, unflattering publicity was having an effect. People were wondering how much longer the vice chancellor could cling to the university's ancient charters.

Confidence oozed from Edwin James as he strode into Westminster Hall that morning. In the intervening months, he'd been busy strengthening his case. Now, on that grey Friday morning, he was ready for battle. Already, he imagined himself taking to the stage to destroy his adversary, Sir Fitzroy Kelly QC, the 64-year-old former Tory MP for Cambridge, who had been engaged to defend the Vice Chancellor of Cambridge University.

Fitzroy Kelly – nicknamed 'apple-pip Kelly' as he had recently argued in a murder case that the deceased had died from eating too many pips – had a reputation for being an agile advocate. Kelly had a large and lucrative private practice, but James had the benefit of the popular press behind him. It would be a bitter fight.

Emma, sitting close to the dock, her gloved hands clasped before her, peered up from beneath the rim of her bonnet to catch every movement. She saw James shuffling pages of notes. She liked this man. He'd won the Cattaway case. He would fight for a second victory against a foe he despised. Her good character would be restored.

Peering round the room, Emma's heart flipped a beat. William Graham, the young man who had invited her to the ill-fated ball so many months ago, sat a little way behind her. He looked older, she thought. The boyishness of his face was gone. Would he tell the truth about that dreadful night, she wondered?

Her thoughts were halted as James, his head held high enough to smooth out the ample chins harnessed into place by the starched tightness of his white collar, took to the stage, where he launched into a long and eloquent speech earning him great praise in the press. First, he took delight in mocking the university for clinging onto its archaic laws. 'There was a time,' he joked, 'when proctors publicly flogged students for bathing in the River Cam, but that custom, having been exercised from time immemorial, has recently been revised.' It was time other ancient laws were revised, he declared. 'At Edinburgh, Glasgow and London there is no such proctorial system, yet I am not aware the morality of those universities is lower than in Cambridge. And such is the local loathing of the powers that street riots and brawls frequently break out.'

Reaching the pinnacle of his performance, he declared, 'It is time the university acted in accordance with the principles of English law and justice. All they do is create bad feeling in the town.'

He then moved on to the plaintiff in the case – Miss Emma Kemp. 'Here is a young woman who proclaimed her innocence when arrested yet was refused the chance of providing evidence of her good character.

She was made to wear a coarse and inferior prison dress, was locked in a cold cell and questioned in the most offensive way. The evidence against her was not heard on oath. During her time in the prison, the vice chancellor was convinced of her innocence. After five days she was liberated. This is not English law,' he triumphantly concluded.

The long-awaited moment arrived. Emma Kemp, the famed dressmaker seeking damages of £500 for false imprisonment, was ushered to the witness box. It had been exactly ten months since she had gathered up her skirts to climb up into the omnibus engaged by William Graham to take her to a ball. Now, as she climbed the steps to fight against the injustice of her arrest, she felt calm and certain truth would prevail.

Graham's eyes followed the girl he had persuaded to attend his ill-fated ball. He watched as she marshalled her skirts once again, this time to climb into the witness stand. Weak daylight fell from the glass dome above her bonneted head.

Edwin James had schooled her in what to expect and how to answer, but her voice faltered at first as he began to put her through her paces. 'My name is … it is Emma Kemp. They call me Emily at home. I have no father. I am a milliner and a dressmaker.'

Her voice gained strength as she heard herself detailing the injustice of the events of the night of 30 January. 'The vice chancellor refused my plea to enquire into my character,' she said. 'I was given a coarse check dress to wear. I was cold. There was no fire in the cell. I did not feel the effects of the cell being heated by hot air coming from the corridor.'

The famous Fitzroy Kelly rose to cross-examine her. 'How long had you known Mr Graham?' he enquired.

'I had known him six months,' Emma replied. 'I met him first at a promenade concert at Fenner's ground. He spoke to me first. I next saw him in the street. I made no appointment to meet him. He invited me to a dancing party when I saw him in the street in the latter part of December.'

'Did you keep a book of the names of those invited to the party?' Kelly was referring to the spiteful letter spliced open by Blore, one of the proctors.

Emma couldn't find an answer at first.

'It was you who found willing dancing partners?' Kelly accused.

Anger ignited Emma. 'I did not. I was not asked to find dancing partners; I was told I could bring someone if I wanted to.'

Kelly paused to press his thin lips together before delivering a line perfectly formed to destroy the plaintiff's character. 'Do you know a young man called Vaughan?'

The question was cruel. Kelly had also used the intervening six months to strengthen his case. He'd sent men out to sniff out every snippet of tittle-tattle that could be used to further damage Emma's character.

Anger warmed Emma's face. Alarm shot through Edwin James. Who is this Vaughan, he wondered?

Emma sucked a breath deep into her lungs. She must stay calm. Mrs Cattaway survived a cruel interrogation – so must she. 'I kept company with him five years ago. I have not seen him for three years.'

'Did you associate with him at the King William the Fourth public house?' asked Kelly.

'I don't know it,' Emma replied.

'It is on the Huntingdon Road,' Kelly reminded her.

There was a pause as distasteful memories of Vaughan trickled into her head and her body stiffened with distaste. 'I was there once,' she recalled.

'Were you found in bed with him when a friend of his came to say he was missed from the university?' Kelly had dealt his master card.

Rage rose inside Emma. She pushed another deep breath into her lungs. 'I swear I was not in a bedroom with Vaughan. I was in a public house with him, but not a bedroom. I was there for about an hour. Not a day or a night more!' Emma barked at Kelly.

'Have you ever had money from Mr Vaughan?' asked Kelly.

'No. No, I have never had money from him.' Tears pricked Emma's eyes. She must stay calm; she must stay calm.

Kelly bounced back for more. 'Mr Lambert, the publican, says you tried to obtain money because you had had a miscarriage.' He seemed to rejoice in hurling damming tittle-tattle at his victim.

The noise inside her head was reaching a kind of boiling point as she steadied herself. Sensing her struggle, James scanned his brain to find a way to rescue her, and the case, from such a punishing interrogation. He could see her gloved hands gripping hard at the slim tube of metal running round the rim of the witness box.

'I did not tell Lambert I had had a miscarriage, nor did I endeavour to obtain money upon that representation.' Emma's voice was rising. 'I get my living by dressmaking,' she said with pride. 'I have never attempted to ask for money from Vaughan or ask for his assistance.'

She attempted to explain what had happened five years ago. 'When I first met Mr Vaughan, he asked where I lived. I gave him the wrong address, as I was afraid of him. Lambert, who keeps carriages, came to me with a fly, more than once, asking me to go with him to meet Vaughan.

He solicited me to meet with Vaughan. I once rode out in a Clarence with Vaughan ...'

Edwin James had had enough. He knew where this line of questioning was going. He went straight to the matter, delivering each word with firm precision. 'At the public house, did anything improper take place?'

'No. No, Sir. There was no connection between us.' Emma was relieved to have the chance to defend the reputation Kelly was determined to destroy.

'And the defence, I see, have called neither man to the witness box.' James's remark dangled in the air until Kelly changed tack.

'Did you tell your mother a lie about where you were going on the night of 30 January?' Kelly coolly asked.

'I had not told my mother any untruth about going to a party, but I had not told her where I was going.'

William Graham was next to be sworn in. 'I am a student at the Inner Temple,' he told James. 'In January last, I had taken my BA degree. On such occasions, there is very often a festivity. I asked the plaintiff to a ball at Shelford.'

His story verified Emma's account. But Kelly wanted to know, 'Did you order breakfast with the intention that the girls would stay all night?' Again, the unverified information in the spiteful letter was driving Kelly's questioning.

'I did not,' Graham said. 'We were all to be home by twelve, according to college regulation. The inn where the party was due to be given was a very respectable establishment.'

'Did anything improper take place between you and the plaintiff?' asked Kelly.

'Nothing improper took place or was planned. I never saw anything about her to show that she was idle, disorderly, or loose in her conduct. I did not treat her as a woman of that character. Milliners and dressmakers often walk about Cambridge, the same as anywhere. It is not unusual to meet them,' Graham said.

The landlady of the De Freville Arms, Mrs Maris, confirmed that no bedrooms had been booked or breakfast ordered.

Mrs Charlotte Locker, Emma's mother, was called. 'The plaintiff is my daughter from my first marriage,' she explained.

Kelly asked, 'And would you have allowed your daughter to go to such a ball as she planned to attend?'

'I would not have suffered it,' Mrs Locker said.

It was now half-past six and the Lord Chief Justice announced his decision to reconvene the next day at ten o'clock.

On the morning of Saturday, 1 December, everyone gathered for the second day of the hearing. It was billed as an important day. It was the day the vice chancellor would face cross-examination in a case brought against him by an alleged prostitute. This was the first time such an eminent member of Cambridge University had been called to court on such a matter.

The Honourable Reverend Latimer Neville's face looked taut as he entered the witness box. Edwin James stood tall. He knew all eyes were on him. Each of his precise questions were delivered with a sneer of contempt.

'Can you tell me why you sentenced Emma Kemp to fourteen days in prison?' he asked.

'I was satisfied the events of that evening were likely to result improperly,' replied a vice chancellor confident he had nothing to hide.

'Why did you authorise her discharge after five days?' pressed James.

'Dr Pulling, the Master of Corpus, told me he employed the mother and believed her to be respectable.'

Edwin James had had to burrow deep to find evidence against the vice chancellor. It was his lax attitude to committal paperwork that provided it. But would it be enough?

'Did you sign the committal document at the time of the arrest?' asked James. 'And had that document already been completed for you. Completed with the sentence, in fact, before you even examined the plaintiff?'

'I cannot say if it was filled in,' fluffed a ruffled vice chancellor, angry that his relaxed attitude was being attacked by outsiders.

'You won't swear it is not in your handwriting?' asked James.

'I can't without seeing it. I don't know whose duty it is to fill in the warrant. I have sometimes done it.'

James wanted to press home his point. It was clear the system was lax, possibly unlawful. There was a flurry. The opposition produced the warrant. James examined it.

'I can't accept this,' James announced. 'It was signed after the committal. Made out in November, although dated January.'

It hinted at the assumption that no one would ever scrutinise the legal procedure inside the Spinning House. Yet the judge accepted the document, despite James's strong objection.

With the case swinging dangerously in favour of the university, James called for an examination of the Elizabethan charter the university claimed gave them the right to arrest and imprison women suspected of 'evil'. He had even gone to the trouble of having it translated from the original Latin.

'This can't be accepted,' Kelly scoffed. 'I have taken advice and this translation is not a correct one.'

The wording was indeed a matter of scholarship. But James wasn't prepared to miss an opportunity. 'The Latin word "*suspectas*" appearing in the original charter refers to women "sometimes suspected",' he explained. 'Women who had been suspected in the past. Thus, any woman arrested must have been "previously suspected" by the proctors and vice chancellor. Therefore, Emma Kemp's arrest was illegal, as she had never before been suspected.' He wanted to make certain this crucial detail was heard.

The Lord Chief Justice refused to allow the translation. James began to wonder if there was any point defending anyone against the power and might of Cambridge University.

It was then the Reverend Mr Blore's turn to be sworn in and give evidence about the letter he had received the previous January warning him about the ball. James called for the letter. A clerk read it aloud and its contents provided a great deal of amusement.

For Emma, however, hearing it for the first time, everything suddenly made sense. Now she understood why she had been singled out for harsher treatment – the spiteful lies implicated her as ringleader! Who could have done this, and why, she wondered?

'Who was the author of the letter?' James asked Blore.

'I have not ascertained who wrote this letter,' he replied.

'It seemed to be in a lady's hand?' questioned James.

'Yes. I took steps to see whether there were any statements that could be verified. It was confirmed that a supper had been ordered,' Blore explained. 'With confirmation the letter contained factual information, I and several other proctors went to meet the omnibus.'

Answering Kelly on cross-examination, he confirmed what he had discovered inside the omnibus that January evening. 'I did not see inside it sufficiently to form an opinion of the young women,' he confessed, 'but knowing it had started from Barnwell, I could not imagine them to be ladies.'

This completed the witness statements. It was time for the summing up. Kelly faced the twelve men of the jury. With the confidence that goes with a lifetime of privilege, he delivered his address.

'The case is an important one, for it concerns the liberty of Her Majesty's subjects,' he began. 'Your decision will affect the morality of thousands of the youth of England. Young men ushered into life to become active members of the community. Men destined to become our generals, our admirals, our statesmen and judges – the very stay of the land. In Cambridge, unusual powers are necessary to protect undergraduates, not so much from the common women of the town as from milliners and dressmakers, girls who at a moment's notice are ready to give their company to a ball or dance. If left unchecked,' he said, 'I fear they would be the ruin of the university.'

Kelly continued, 'Here were a number of young men in their hey-day of youth, in the heat of blood, consorting together for midnight revelry of the lowest condition, not at a private house, but at a public house where there would be dancing and drinking. Their passions excited by wine,' he warned, 'it was bound to end in immorality. It had been the duty of the proctors to act on the letter. And it is those women who avoid the public gaze who are more dangerous than the common prostitute because they seduce young men, entangle them.' Worse, he stated, 'they prevent them from applying assiduously to their studies'. Looking full in the faces of those sitting in the jury box, he implored them, 'Do not lend your hands to pulling down a barrier of protection for young men about to take up positions of importance in our land.'

Edwin James stuck to the legal facts in his summary. 'The decision of the jury will have a very important effect on the proctorial system at Cambridge. Indeed, I hope that in future it will be carried out properly according to the law of the land. The university are not above the control of any court of justice in England. The guilty escape and the innocent are punished.' It was his belief, he said, that 'the anonymous letter providing so much of the evidence was written by a young woman "disappointed" of an invitation'. He quipped, 'My friend talks of generals, judges and admirals who were brought up at the university, but I should like to see any ermined judge or lawn-sleeved bishop who could swear he had not in his youth had a flirtation with a milliner's girl in their day. And,' he proclaimed, 'I would not think the worse of him either for such behaviour. But we must be jealous of the liberty of the subject to see that the university does not abuse it. They must exercise their power in moderation. Perhaps it is time for an Act of Parliament to sweep away their powers.'

Soft cries of 'Hear, hear!' spread around the room. A triumphant James had to stop himself bowing to his appreciative audience as he returned to his seat.

The Lord Chief Justice explained to the jury that their job was to consider two points. First, did the proctors have reasonable grounds to suspect the plaintiff of immoral behaviour, and second, did the vice chancellor have reasonable grounds to imprison Emma Kemp?

The jury retired to a private room to deliberate.

All of those present knew just how important the outcome of the jury's deliberations would be. Emma Kemp and the vice chancellor were fighting for their reputations. Everything hung in the balance for the entire hour and thirty minutes those dozen men spent pondering on the rights and wrongs of the situation. Little did either know the role that a man from the plantations of Demerara would play in determining the outcome of the trial.

12

AN UNUSUAL LAW

The deliberations of a jury are not recorded, yet it is possible to imagine how the debate unfolded when one delves into the characters of the members of that jury. Each of the twelve men of the special jury selected to hear *Kemp vs Neville* are listed as being London merchants or esquires, and each was relived to retire from the increasing discomfort of the hard wooden seats of the jury box. The move to a private room behind the Court of Common Pleas gave them a chance to straighten their limbs and declare bafflement at the task they were about to untangle.

The foreman of the jury, the most senior man present, Philp Worsley, took charge. A brewer by trade, he was now a partner at Whitbread Brewery and lived at 4 Taviton Street, Bloomsbury, with his wife, four children and a handful of servants.

'The eyes of many are on us,' he said, as he brought the men to order. 'The law in Cambridge is unusual. We must take our time to consider the facts.'

A murmur of agreement was heard.

'She's broken no law, as far as I see it,' uttered George James Clifton, a wine merchant born in Demerara, now residing in some splendour in Marylebone. Clifton had recently been compensated for freeing over 100 slaves from his father's West Indies estate. 'She was unwise to involve her young sister, but that's all I can condemn her for,' he reflected, to the agreement of the rest of the jury.

'We can't ignore the fact that in Cambridge it is lawful to arrest "suspicious" women,' Worsley reminded Clifton. 'The first question is, do we find the proctors had reasonable grounds to suspect Emma Kemp of immoral behaviour?'

The anonymous letter – addressed to Blore – detailing the plans for the clandestine ball was discussed. 'Her downfall,' Clifton said. The spite of the letter rankled with him. As a wine merchant, he wasn't impressed by the powers Cambridge University extended over the tradesmen in Cambridge. He knew that while the students were eager to fill their wine cellars and wardrobes and smoke cigars, their tutors acted against tradesmen who allowed the young men to run up debts. He was not a man to side with the outdated powers of the university.

The men agreed that once the proctors had discovered information in the letter held some truth, reasonable grounds existed for suspicion, but further inquiries should have been made. The letter stated where she lived; questions could have been asked.

'Quite, quite,' said Clifton. 'She was released as soon as the vice chancellor discovered the family was a respectable one. He was negligent.'

'The evidence shows the girl was innocent, but foolish,' Worsley agreed.

'True,' Edward Nettleford, a merchant living in Albion Road, Newington, chipped in. 'Graham believed her to be respectable. He confirmed breakfast was never ordered, despite it being hinted at in the letter. But the girl knew she shouldn't have gone. She kept it a secret from her mother. And should not have taken her 14-year-old sister with her.'

A good deal of discussion followed about the law of the land. A charge could only be made if there was proof of soliciting. In Cambridge, women could be arrested and imprisoned for being 'suspected of evil'. But that was the law only in Cambridge. How could they judge a case where the judge recognised the legality of another law?

Worsley took out his pocket watch. Time was ticking by. An hour had passed, yet they were no closer to solving the conundrum.

'What about the damages?' asked Nettleford. 'They are high. We agree she acted foolishly.'

The men agreed that Emma had acted irresponsibly. An offer of £25 was agreed to reflect her part in the sorry story.

But the men couldn't find a way of answering the judge's question about the vice chancellor. They all agreed he should have made enquiries about the character of the plaintiff.

'Let's stick to the law of the land,' an irritated Clifton eventually proposed. 'This is an English court not the vice chancellor's courtroom.' He'd came up with a plan. One that would cause bafflement and confusion for months to come.

The court clerk made it known the jury were ready. This was the moment Emma, her mother, Cockerell, Edwin James and so many others had been waiting for. Would the world-famous educational institution be forced to embrace the modern workings of the modern world?

Emma watched the twelve men file into the jury box. She saw the foreman hand a piece of paper to the court clerk. He noticed bafflement freeze the clerk's face as the foreman bent close to his ear to pass on a piece of information.

Quizzical glances were exchanged as the Lord Chief Justice gazed at the inky words on the paper before him. He lifted his eyes upwards as if seeking divine assistance. He examined the words for a second time. 'Would the foreman of the jury stand!' called out the clerk.

Philip Worsley rose to his feet. The jury exchanged glances.

'You find that the proctors had reasonable grounds for suspicion,' the Lord Chief Justice stated.

'We do,' Worsley replied.

All seemed to be going well for the defence. Emma prepared for bad news. The Lord Chief Justice, once again, flicked his eyes towards the ceiling. Everyone sensed a problem. Many shuffled to the edge of their seat, willing their eyes and ears to pick up every moment of what might be about to happen.

'You say ...' the Lord Chief Justice hesitantly started. 'You say that the vice chancellor did not make enquiries into the character of the plaintiff.' He paused again. 'You say the punishment was undeserved. I didn't put a direct question about whether the vice chancellor had made due enquiry. I asked if he had reasonable grounds to imprison the plaintiff. Perhaps you mean the vice chancellor had reasonable grounds for suspicion, the same as the proctors?'

'Certainly not.' It was Clifton who volunteered the answer. 'The proctors had reasonable grounds, not the vice chancellor.'

'This is the meaning of your finding?' asked the Lord Chief Justice.

'It is,' replied Worsley.

Another juror spoke up. 'The vice chancellor didn't make enquiries about the girl, which we believe, under the circumstances, was necessary.'

'This does not answer my question or amount to a verdict,' declared the Lord Chief Justice. He loudly hammered out the question again. 'Was the vice chancellor right to believe the proctors in thinking the plaintiff was in the company of undergraduates for the purpose of idle, immoral and disorderly purposes?'

Worsley asked, 'If we find this to be true will it be a verdict for the defendant?

'Yes,' said the Lord Chief Justice.

'We cannot agree then.'

The Lord Chief Justice was furious. Under the terms of the Elizabethan charter, whose law was the law in Cambridge, the vice chancellor could imprison women he had reasonable grounds to 'suspect' of 'evil'. The anonymous letter was proof enough under the terms of the ancient charter. But the jury insisted on judging the case according to the law of the land. Where was the evidence that Emma Kemp had immoral intentions?

'I must send you back to reconsider your verdict,' ordered the Lord Chief Justice. 'You must recognise the unusual laws that exist in Cambridge.'

The twelve men, as instructed, returned to the room to deliberate.

This was a tricky legal matter. The jury was judging the matter according to the law of the land, but the judge needed to consider the laws and privileges conferred on the university under the ancient Elizabethan charter – which were also the law. To prove Emma was a prostitute, which this case had hinged on, the law of the land required evidence, not hearsay. The jury felt quite able to agree that the anonymous letter gave the proctors reason to suspect the ball was 'got up' for immoral purposes, but on the other hand, the vice chancellor, under the law of the land, should have asked for evidence as to the character and reputation of Emma Kemp before sentencing her to two weeks in prison. The jury could not find the vice chancellor innocent.

After half an hour, the jury returned. 'We cannot say yes or no to the proposition placed before us,' Worsley explained. 'We all agree that further enquiry should have been made before the girl was imprisoned.'

'I think it is no use sending the jury back to reconsider?' questioned the Lord Chief Justice.

'Certainly not,' chorused the jurors. 'The majority would not agree to that.'

'In that case,' sighed the Lord Chief Chancellor, 'I will enter a verdict for the plaintiff, but at the same time, I state that in my opinion it is an imperfect verdict. As for the damages, I award £25.'

It was a verdict that crushed hopes for justice. The power of the proctors to arrest women on the grounds of 'suspicion' had been proven in an English court, but the right of the vice chancellor to arbitrarily imprison women had been successfully challenged. It was hard to comprehend such an outcome.

After months of undesirable publicity and expensive fees, the university had nothing to celebrate. Emma's name had been cleared of wrongdoing yet doubts about her character stuck in the minds of the 'great and good' in Cambridge. There had been no winners in *Kemp vs Neville*. But Fitzroy Kelly could not let it rest there. The end had not yet arrived. Under Kelly's direction, an appeal against the judgment was lodged by the university.

In June 1861, the case dragged to its tortuous conclusion. Following great debate over the exact wording of the Latin charter, the Lord Chief Justice set aside the original verdict. He entered instead for the defendant. But, as *The Times* newspaper noted the following day, the university had scented danger. Arrests, sentencing and the completion of paperwork inside the Spinning House were revised. Caution was the word.

Back in Barnwell, it wasn't many months before Mrs Locker and Emma were taking in washing to make ends meet.

Latimer Neville, Master of Magdalene College and vice chancellor 1859–61, would go down in history for being a 'dull man, lacking intellectual powers', famous only for *Kemp vs Neville*, under which it was firmly established that the proctors still had the right to arrest and imprison women 'suspected of evil'.

Emma Kemp would be forever remembered as the innocent young woman whose determination to clear her name resulted in the gradual dismantling of the power of the university to arrest women. From that day, arrests plummeted. But as the townspeople went about their daily business, university dons wrangled to change a decree that would change everything.

THE SPINNING HOUSE.
Cambridge.

FOUNDED 1628.

ABOLISHED 1894.

Front Entrance.

The Spinning House (Museum of Cambridge Collection).

No. 557 Name, &c.	Date of Apprehension.	Present Residence.	By whom apprehended.
Mary Clark	May 11. 44.	8 Burleigh St.	Mr. Hildyard
	Feb. 18th/45		Mr. Thackeray
Age 23 Parish Barnwell	March 10th		
No 740	April 15th		
	25 Novr/45		Mr. Edleston
Parents or Friends } Mother Laundress	Decr. 7.		Mr. Humphry
	May /46		Mr. Humphry
	Octr 21. 1846	28. Burleigh Street	Mr. Brummel
Last Situation living with her mother	Novr 13. 46		Mr. Saunders
	Novr 25.		Mr. Saunders
	Decr 3 46		Mr. Saunders
	Febr 1. 47		Mr. Kingsley

No. 558 Elizabeth Howe	May 12/44	#7 Union Row	Mr. Dodd
	Oct 31		Mr. Gordon
Age 19 Parish Foulmire	Mar 12/46		Mr. Edleston
	May 9/46		Mr. Humphry
Parents or Friends } Father & Mother at Foulmire Sister can attend to this	Nov 6/46		Mr. Kingsley
Last Situation Miss Milner Parkers as servant			

Committal of Elizabeth Howe (reproduced by kind permission of the Syndics of Cambridge University Library).

THE

SPINNING HOUSE

ABOMINATION.

Title page of Henry Mayhew's *The Spinning House Abomination 1851* (Cambridgeshire Collection).

Court Yard & Exterior of Cells.

The exercise courtyard of the Spinning House (Museum of Cambridge Collection).

The Cells 1st Floor.

The Spinning House cells, 1st Floor (Museum of Cambridge Collection).

The Cells 2nd Floor.

The Spinning House cells, 2nd Floor (Museum of Cambridge Collection).

eagle, in the poet's figure, recognised the shaft that
brought it death as one from its own wing, but the
shaft from Labby's quiver did not deal its owner
harm.

THE SPINNING HOUSE.

The Proctorial fraternity at Cambridge no doubt
rubbed their hands in high glee when they heard
that "Daisy Hopkins, the Heroine of the Spinning
House Scandal," had been locked up in London on a

DAISY HOPKINS.

charge of drunken and disorderly conduct. Unfortunately for their hopes and fears it appears that
Miss Hopkins had been personated by some worthless
character, who had given the name of the now well-
known martyr to the cause of the Spinning House,
and that the real Daisy Hopkins had never been
away from her home on the day in question. It is
gratifying, therefore, to those who wish to see the
Spinning House swept away that the Proctors will
not have this case to put forward in justification of
their precious institution. The real Miss Daisy
Hopkins, whose portrait is here given, has served
the pro-Proctor with a writ of action for wrongful
imprisonment and malicious prosecution, claiming
£1,000 damages. The case will be heard at the next
Norwich Assizes.

OSCAR WILDE MAKES A HIT.

Mr. Oscar Wilde has not disappointed the expectations of his admirers. He has achieved a
genuine dramatic success in "Lady Windermere's
Fan." The play was produced last Saturday night

Daisy Hopkins – a sketch from the *Nantwich Guardian* – Saturday, 27 February 1892
(Cambridgeshire Collection).

PROCTOR, *in Congregation habit. The ruff, a broad band of silk, pleated, is worn by the Senior Proctor over the right shoulder and under the left, and by the Junior Proctor under the right shoulder and over the left, so that when they stand together in the Senate House it makes a complete yoke. He carries the Statutes of the University, being responsible for the discipline of Undergraduates and Bachelors.*

A Proctor (Cambridgeshire Collection).

13

A REBELLIOUS DAUGHTER

Jane (Kate) Elsden

Age: 17
Arrested: 27 January 1891, 11 February 1891
Recaptured: 14 February 1891
Arresting proctor: The Reverend Reginald St John Parry
Charge: Talking to a member of the university; street walking; jail breaking
Sentence: Two weeks; three weeks; remainder of her sentence

n 1880, much of the town rhythmically rang with the sound of hammers. Cambridge resembled a building site. Bricks were being baked and carted at a rate never seen before. The hammering and baking followed a revision of the statutes. The same year, it was confirmed that fellows could now marry without forfeiting their fellowship.

A small revolution had occurred. In no time at all, spacious family villas lined new airy roads on the leafy edges of town. It was here that the first hatching of university families emerged. Cambridge would never be the same again.

Local men were accruing small fortunes. Department stores were stretching into neighbouring buildings. Builders' yards doubled in size, as did the homes of newly wealthy tradesmen. Cambridge born, bred and educated young men took up professions in the town. Fellows and their wives started taking an interest in the place their children called home. And into this new world tumbled the conflicting characters of Jane Elsden and Montague Butler. The final battle to remove every dusty brick of the dreaded Spinning House prison was about to begin.

It was the summer of 1888 when the lively brown-eyed Jane Elsden arrived in Cambridge to begin her adult life. She was 15 years old, the eldest of seven children in a family of little means. She'd nursed her mother, cradled her infant siblings, been chastised for poor attendance at school and teased for stuffing moss in the soles of her ill-fitting boots. Primed to challenge every sideways glance and defend the honour of a family struggling to make ends meet, she knew on reaching 15 she could no longer burden the household purse.

Her education had been as inadequate as her chances of securing employment in rural Suffolk – the place she'd first called home. The lives of working-class women are barely documented, so we can only guess what this slim, attractive, undereducated young woman with dark gold hair might have done for money. But no one could have predicted that three years later, this feisty teenager would be hailed as a martyr to the cause of freedom in the national newspapers. And the man who'd imprisoned her, twice, in the Spinning House, would be forced to yield.

The prospects of the Elsden children should have been better. The Education Act of 1870 made schooling compulsory. But when Jane travelled to Cambridge to start her new life, she left an ailing mother battling to cope with the drudgery of domestic duties. Fewer and fewer ticks appeared against her siblings' names on the school register. More and more black marks stacked up.

Three times after Jane's departure, her father Walter Elsden was summoned to the Petty Sessions at Newmarket Magistrates' Court, accused of neglecting his children's education. On the fourth occasion, it was his wife Catherine who covered the ground between Dullingham and the famous horseracing town to stand before the magistrate. The school board inspector, Mr Charles Westley, provided rows of blank squares as evidence of absence and complained to the magistrate, 'The children never attended regularly, despite the parents having already been fined.'

Mrs Elsden's facial contortions betrayed the seething rage inside her. Like her daughter, she was easily unsettled by injurious remarks. 'I'll send my children to school when I can!' she burst out. 'But when I'm ill, I'll keep them away.'

'But they must attend regularly,' the school inspector patiently reminded her.

'And why,' she indignantly demanded, 'does the school inspector not go after other people who never send their children to school at all? Instead of always looking after me?'

The magistrate wearily issued a further fine, this time doubling it to 5s. As Mrs Elsden bustled out of the witness box, her pent-up sentiments exploded into angry words. 'In future I will send my children to the stone pits and then if I am fined again at least they will be earning their own fines!'

Jane Elsden arrived in a town that was greatly changed from the one Elizabeth Howe had arrived in, in similar circumstances, over forty years before. She lodged in a room in Kettle's Yard, on the northern edge of Cambridge in the Castle End area – a part of the town notorious for its poverty and vice.

Kettle's Yard was a dank place where twenty-six tiny cottages squeezed into a place suitable for none. Nine years before, these homes had been described by health officials as 'fever dens'. Its inhabitants drew their drinking water from a pump in the churchyard of St Giles Church, where the water filtered itself through the corpses of the dead and buried. Consuming beer at one of the eleven public houses wedged among the yards, rows and hills of dilapidated houses was a better option.

Most of the women in Castle End worked as laundresses, washing undergraduates' linen at home, spreading it out to dry on the 'Green Hills', as the grassy banks in nearby Mount Pleasant, once the ramparts of an ancient Roman fort, were fondly named.

Jane escaped her mother's bidding when she moved to Cambridge, but it wasn't long before she followed in her footsteps as a courtroom entertainer. The quarrelsome melodrama of her new urban life first unfolded in the 'Police Intelligence' section of the *Cambridge Independent*.

Jane was a kind, attractive, feisty young woman, whose independence drew people to her, but her popularity inspired spite, and the antics of catty women, as seen in the case of Emma Kemp, could be the undoing of any woman. Jane's notoriety began when rows and reconciliations between her and her infamous Castle End neighbour, Annie Woodroffe, kicked off. The pair got drunk together, disagreed together and made up together, only to disagree again.

The alcoholic haze she sought so often blotted out the sadness of her lonely life – and Annie's, too. Quarrels marked the highs and lows of their enduring friendship as they slipped in and out of the Rose and Tulip public house in St Andrew's Street. It was at the Rose and Tulip – its long, dark side passage was known as a 'harbour' for women sheltering from the gaze of the proctors – where Jane and Annie had their first notable skirmish. It was in October 1888, when an enraged Annie – we don't know what misdeed had been committed – spotted Jane approaching the Rose and Tulip. Annie concealed herself in the shadows of the pub's infamous passage, coiled to launch an attack on her 'friend'. As the unsuspecting Jane passed by, Annie spat out a torrent of bad language. Jane ignored her taunts, and not provoking the quarrel she craved, Annie upped the stakes.

'Want a fight?' she taunted. 'Winner takes ten shillings off the other. Meet me on the common [Parker's Piece] later.'

'Leave off!' Jane replied, hurrying past her usual haunt. She didn't want trouble.

But when the friends' paths crossed later that night, a further tirade of filthy language and threats of violence were hurled at Jane. Shaken and frightened, Jane went to the police station to press charges against Annie.

It wasn't difficult for the law to find a young woman burdened with a history of drunken disorder guilty; it was, after all, Annie's third charge of using obscene language in the street and her seventh offence in Cambridge. Fourteen days in prison followed and Jane Elsden's first entry into the Cambridge courts had been recorded.

The Rose and Tulip became known as the place to find the increasingly argumentative, now 16-year-old, Jane as she defended her right to fair treatment – she couldn't help it if a young man looked her way. It was here, a year later, that an angry Albert Campion found her. He wanted a word with Jane Elsden. Annie, thrilled by the promise of trouble, stuck close to her friend.

'You've done a nice thing telling Mrs Jackson about me,' Campion said.

'I did nothing,' Jane replied, knowing exactly what she had done. A few days before, she had spotted Campion stealing a portrait from a house nearby. He hadn't spotted her and Jane, who had turned tell-tale to a very grateful Mrs Jackson, who had then turned tell-tale on her.

'I could break your **** head!' he threatened.

Jane let out a vindictive snigger as she delivered some catty observations about Albert's girlfriend, Florrie Hume, standing by his side. Cloaked in masculine rage, he lunged at Jane. 'I'll ring your nose for that,' he hissed.

Jane took a step backward, readying her fists. Annie, sensing immediate injury to her friend, grabbed hold of her.

'Quick!' Annie ordered as she pulled Jane along in the direction of the police station. 'We'll say he tried to assault you.'

When the case came to court, it was Annie who verified the violent verbal attack. Albert Campion was fined 3s and Jane Elsden's name appeared in the Cambridge court records for a second time.

The following month, Jane woke up in hospital after a severe assault by another Annie – Annie Davis – who had taken exception to her 'undue intimacy' with her estranged husband. The jealous 24-year-old had grabbed Jane. Punches flew until Annie succeeded in slamming Jane to the ground. From there, she jumped on Jane's defenceless body until she passed out.

A fearful Annie Woodroffe sat with her friend on the pavement, waiting to see if she regained consciousness. When she did, she helped Jane limp off to the police station to press charges against Annie Davis. By then, Jane was almost hysterical with the pain.

A doctor was immediately sent for. Her ailing body was rushed to Addenbrooke's Hospital in Trumpington Street in a fly. It was 11.30 in the evening when the house surgeon, Mr Ashton Street, examined Jane's battered body. He found half a dozen bruises on the right side of her face and two scratches on the left. She was in great pain at the back of her head and in her lower abdomen.

A sleeping draught was prescribed which brought her a good night's sleep, but when she woke on Saturday morning she was still racked with pain. The surgeon performed an operation on her abdomen. We don't know the full details, but it worked. Jane was discharged on Monday.

Annie Davis was charged with assault and spent a month in prison.

But it wasn't long before tipsy street fights and catty revenge wore down Jane's resolve to stay on the right side of the law. Two years after her arrival in Cambridge, she found herself in court, this time defending a complaint of assault.

Prison awaited her in October 1890 when she was in court once again. Ever volatile, her anger had boiled over on catching sight of a friend walking past The Wrestlers public house in Newmarket Road, where Jane was enjoying a glass of beer. A few weeks before, a quarrel between them had seen Jane forced out of the pony and trap transporting her and that friend back to Cambridge, following a day out at the races in Newmarket.

Jane had a fondness for holding a grudge. Tumbling out of The Wrestlers, Jane shouted across the road, 'Why did you leave me in that dirty way? I had to walk all the way home!'

Words turned to blows. Two pairs of hands flew to find and pull handfuls of hair and booted feet kicked out. Customers inside the pub rushed out to separate the bruised and bloodied brawlers.

In court, each blamed the other. But it was the petite, brown-haired Jane Elsden who was found guilty of causing bodily harm, despite the opinion of one of the magistrates that she appeared to have come off worse. Jane was likeable, in spite her uncommunicative ways. Her vulnerability wasn't invisible to everyone who encountered her.

The outburst cost her six weeks in the town jail and coincided with the renewed vigour of the newly installed vice chancellor – The Very Reverend Henry Montague Butler – whose mission it was to 'clean' the streets of suspicious young women, due to fears expressed in *The Times* by anxious mothers of sons destined for Cambridge. 'What will our sons be exposed to if they go up to Cambridge?' worried one mother.

Arrests doubled as Butler ordered his men to show no mercy. And, on leaving the town prison, Jane Elsden had become a person of interest.

The 44-year-old widowed Latinist Montague Butler, Master of Trinity College, hadn't had to worry about missing school or making ends meet. But he had gained a kind of fame in 1888 when he married 21-year-old Agnata Ramsey.

Agnata was the celebrated Girton College girl who, in 1887, was the only candidate in the entire university to achieve a first-class distinction in the Classics Tripos. The famous couple were feted in high society and the world of academia. Despite soon becoming a mother, Mrs Butler managed to complete her edition of *Herodotus*, but was disappointed to have to resign her appointment as Classical tutor at Girton on her marriage. The couple's eldest child was nicknamed the 'Unique baby'– the only baby in the world who had a senior classicist for both its father and mother.

Distracted by his celebrated new life, Butler was chastised by the Master of Downing College for 'weakening the hunt for "evil" women'. Many parents feared working-class girls were temptresses who would pollute the morals of their precious sons. It was the vice chancellor's duty to soothe their nerves.

Suitably rebuked, Butler ordered his proctors to greater vigilance. Weekly, term-time only meetings were held to swap notes about young women who had been warned or arrested. It was a step in the right direction for some, but not for Jane Elsden. Her release from prison made her a target for the proctors' harsher regime. After two years of unruly behaviour on the streets, the 17-year-old had become a person the proctors wanted off the streets of Cambridge.

Trinity Lane, the narrow street squeezed between the high walls of Trinity College and Gonville and Caius College, offered a degree of concealment from the night-time prying of the proctor and his men. A uniform row of towering, smoking chimneys further clouded the moonlight from shining on the cobbles below.

It was in this little lane, on the evening of Tuesday, 27 January 1891, that Jane Elsden decided to lurk when her supply of money dwindled to nothing. It wasn't long before a scholar spotted her. Deep in conversation, neither noticed the silent advancement of the proctor and his Bulldogs. In no time at all, heavy hands landed on Jane's slim shoulders.

'You're coming with us,' a Bulldog announced.

'I'm not doing anything!' she snapped as she wriggled to free herself.

Under the terms of the ancient charter, she was guilty. She'd been found in the company of a gownsman. But according to the law of the land, she was innocent – and she knew it. 'We're only talking!' she shouted. 'You've no proof of anything else!' But her fate was as sure as the strong arms preventing her escape.

'Come quietly,' the proctor, Reginald St John Parry of Trinity College, urged.

Jane knew where she was bound. It was her first time inside the dreaded building. The smell and feel of damp weaved its way through the cold, fusty rooms and into her body as her details were entered in the third volume of the Spinning House Committal Books. There was nothing she could do but comply, despite the anger burning inside her.

The next morning, the vice chancellor arrived to hear the case against her. Jane stood before the gowned figure of Montague Butler. St John Parry, the arresting proctor, related the facts that, according to the charter, could only condemn her. She had been found in the company of a member of the university.

Montague Butler surveyed her. 'Did she come quietly?' he enquired.

'No,' said the proctor.

Barely blinking, Butler handed Jane a fourteen-day sentence. She was powerless. Jutting her chin in rage and locking in her mouth all the things she wanted to scream as she totted up the rent she would owe on her release, she succumbed to the injustice. But inside, she seethed.

She lived in a country whose laws protected the liberty of its citizens, yet the detested charter clearly stated that women 'suspected' of soliciting could be locked away. Somehow, Jane would get her revenge.

The Spinning House was cold and damp compared to the town prison Jane had so recently resided in, but she used those two weeks to gather useful information about the habits and routines of Agnes, the under matron. The next time the Bulldogs laid their hands on Jane Elsden, she would make certain things turned out differently.

14

THE RUNAWAY

It was two weeks and a day later, when the town clocks began striking eleven, that Jane Elsden breathed in freedom as she ambled along the gaslit streets of Cambridge. She felt good. The night was still as it slipped towards sleep. A damp fenland mist was stretching its lingering fingers into every crevice of the town. But Jane was in no rush as she turned into Petty Cury on her way to the Market Square, in the centre of Cambridge. There, she spotted the shadowy outline of three men coming towards her. Fear filled her. It was the proctor and men on their nightly patrol. She knew she must flee, but the men had spotted her. The chase was on.

Gripping her shawl tightly in one hand while desperately clasping up her long skirts with the other, 17-year-old Jane ran as fast as her clothing would permit. She knew the terrain, darting into an adjoining street in search of refuge in one of its tight alleys. Then she sought invisibility in the shadows of the Prince of Wales Passage, where she paused to suck more air into her heaving lungs, her bodice restricting every breath.

But the Bulldogs knew the dark passages as well as their prey. Guessing her route, they formed a pincer movement, ensnaring the petrified girl as she emerged from what she had hoped was the shadow of safety. Grabbing her, they pinned her flailing arms against the wall.

'Get off me!' she panted.

'The proctor wants you,' one of the Bulldogs said, pressing her harder against the wall. There the trio waited a few moments until the proctor arrived. Peering at her flushed, angry face, he immediately recognised her. The gloom of the back streets hadn't diminished the handsome face and long, brown hair now escaping its fastening under her tightly secured hat. He remembered the spirited struggle as she tried to wriggle out of being arrested, two weeks before.

'You,' he said, 'are to come with me.'

'I won't!' she cried out, raising her elbows with the intention of loosening the iron grip holding her. 'I wasn't with anyone; you can't take me!' she shouted. With no sign of escape, she changed tack. 'I'm not with any university men,' she pleaded.

It had only been thirty hours since her release from the Spinning House, where she had served a two-week sentence for being found talking to an undergraduate in Trinity Lane – a crime unknown outside the powerful reaches of Cambridge and Oxford Universities. She seethed with rage. There was no law against this. It wasn't right. It wasn't fair.

'What am I accused of?' she demanded.

No reply came.

As the men tried to force her forward, she refused to let her legs comply. The Bulldogs pushed and pulled her along St Andrew's Street. She harangued them with every insult she could muster.

Within fifteen minutes, Jane was shoved through the heavy wooden doors of the Spinning House, wincing at the sound of bolts and locks sliding into place behind her.

Agnes Grey, the under matron, who virtually ran the prison, was startled to be so soon reunited with a prisoner she had been privately pleased to say farewell to. Escorting the party to the usual room beyond the inner courtyard, she prepared pen and ink for the proctor, who took down the latest Committal Book. Pushing back the sleeves of his academic gown, he inked in the prisoner's details on a sheet of stiff, waxy, cream-coloured paper. Only the sound of his scratching pen broke the silence in the small whitewashed room.

It didn't break Jane. She had been arrested for walking the streets for the purpose of 'evil', despite there being no evidence to support this nor it being against the ordinary law. Her blazing anger provided the only warmth in the cold and damp cell she was forced into. But she had no intention of staying a prisoner for long.

The Spinning House matron, Mrs Agnes Johnson, had replaced Mr Wilson, the male keeper, thirty-seven years ago. Her face was now framed with grey and her legs had become unwilling to transport her beyond the prison walls.

Matron's only experience of the world outside was what could be gleaned from others. She'd heard about the trickle of well-to-do young ladies taking up residence at the two new women's colleges founded in Girton, in 1869, and Newnham in 1871. By 1880, the trickle had eased sufficiently for the university to issue strict rules curtailing the freedom of the 'nasty forward minxes', as Professor Adam Sedgwick, an unmarried Fellow of Trinity College, labelled them. The young women learnt to make themselves as small and invisible as possible for fear of giving offence to those whose hearts and minds were against them.

The 'minxes' could not take part in university life and suffered many restrictions. 'We must always wear gloves in the town, and of course hats,' complained Catherine Dampier, one of the early cohorts of Newnham College students, to her mother. 'We are not allowed to ride or cycle in the main streets or take a boat out on the river in the daytime unless accompanied by a chaperone.'

Matron had learnt of the fellows' wives who'd taken an interest in providing training schools to teach young women in the town who'd been identified as being at risk of 'falling' how to become dutiful servants. Matron wondered how secure her job might be.

Yet the likes of Jane Elsden had no one to protect them from being a magnet of suspicion for the proctor and his men, however fair or unfair that might be. It was eleven o'clock, the morning after Jane's second arrest, when she appeared before Butler for a second time. The trial, back in the room the two had met in just over two weeks ago, lasted no more than fifteen minutes. Jane listened as the proctor relayed the details of her crime.

'She was found walking the streets for the purpose of "evil",' said Parry.

'Did she come quietly?' Butler asked.

'No.'

Taking a long look at the girl in front of him, he wondered what he could do to deter such an unfortunate character. A note of fatherly regret was detected in Butler's voice as he informed the prisoner, 'I am sorry, but we shall detain you here for three weeks.'

Three weeks! It made no sense. It was so unfair; so unjust. This same man had delivered her a two-week sentence a little over a fortnight ago for talking to a member of the university. This time she'd done nothing wrong. Nothing. Broken no known law. Aflame with rage, she didn't, in fact couldn't, hold back. 'I always thought England was a free country!' she yelled. 'But I find it is not.'

Powerless against university authority, despite her arrest being illegal in the outside world, there was nothing she could do. Agnes returned her to her cell. But the seething Jane had the knowledge of an insider and had no intention of suffering inside that prison one moment more.

During her previous stay, the cunning and resourceful girl had studied Agnes's little routines. Unseen, she had quietly turned doorknobs, finding how effortlessly some doors opened; how easy it might be to slip away. It was 4.30 in the quiet routine of the afternoon when Jane rang the bell to summon the under matron. 'Please might I get some fresh air?'

The under matron wasn't sure. 'Just try to rest,' she suggested.

'I've got a bad head,' Jane pleaded.

Kindness overtook Agnes. She escorted Jane outside to the small exercise yard at the rear of the prison. It didn't provide a great deal of fresh air because a row of lofty houses overlooked the yard. An odour of waste was ever present. But it wasn't fresh air Jane was seeking.

'I'll be back soon,' Agnes kindly told her.

Jane already knew exactly how long Agnes would be away and where she was going. The under matron was off to post her letters. Jane had fifteen minutes to carry out the plan she had been hatching since the vice chancellor had dealt his cruel blow.

Alone in the prison yard, she chose that moment to make her escape. Slipping through doors so carelessly left unlocked, she found her way to the chaplain's room, on the ground floor. Here, she climbed up to the window. She tore aside a blind and, releasing the window catch, nimbly she squeezed her small frame through the narrow gap and jumped down onto the pavement below to freedom.

She was back in St Andrew's Street, but she didn't stop to linger. Penniless and alone, she fled the 15 miles back to the safety of her family home in Dullingham. However, she was not to enjoy the peace of rural life for long.

When news of the escape reached Butler, he was incandescent with fury. Over the last few decades, only a handful of women had escaped from the Spinning House. Previous vice chancellors had shrugged their shoulders, but Butler would not let it rest. Immediately, he took the unprecedented step of ordering the university solicitor, Musgrave Francis, to scour the ancient statutes to find a clause permitting him to rearrest the runaway.

Francis found one but noted that Butler didn't have the power to try anyone for prison breaking. Only a local magistrate could do that.

Francis was mindful of the frenzy a public hearing could cause. Times had changed and the ancient statutes of the university had not caught up. Butler wasn't aware of the strength of feeling against his authority to imprison women who hadn't broken the law, yet he demanded retribution – a decision he would regret.

And so it was, on Saturday, 14 February, that Police Constable George Johnson arrived in Dullingham clutching a warrant for Jane's arrest. She was looking out of an upstairs window and spotted him coming in the direction of their cottage and called out, 'You want me?'

Constable Johnson did want her.

'I'm not dressed,' she teased, 'so you can't take me.'

Jane was wearing nothing but a skirt over her under linen, but she hastily flung on her father's old Ulster coat to project her modesty as she tripped downstairs to open the door and explain to PC Johnson why he couldn't take her.

'My clothes are being washed,' she declared. 'I can't come.'

'Get away! She can't come,' came another voice. It was an enraged Mrs Elsden.

Wash day was not going to deter the constable from his duty. He moved forward to grasp her arm.

'You've no right to take her!' Mrs Elsden's indignation filled the doorway.

'I'm not going back!' Jane shouted.

'I'm here to take you to the county jail. It's the magistrate who wants to see you,' he explained. 'You're to be tried for prison breaking.'

This was different. Despite the enraged protests of mother and daughter, suitable clothing was found.

Later that Saturday afternoon, Jane was back in custody in Cambridge. But Montague Butler had slipped up. He could not have known the extent to which his high-handed actions would be condemned.

15

BRITISH LAW

On the morning of Monday, 16 February, Jane was back in Cambridge. Not as a resident of nearby Kettle's Yard, but in the Police Court on Castle Hill. The old gatehouse of the castle had long been demolished, making way for an impressive new court. Everyone entering its loggia-fronted arches passed under four towering statues symbolising justice and liberty.

This courtroom could not have been more different from the small whitewashed room where Butler had twice sentenced Jane to a term of imprisonment, despite her not breaking the law of the land. Here, a narrow wooden gallery seated those curious to catch sight of the 'notorious' Jane Elsden and enjoy a town and gown row.

The town rose to the occasion of the spectacle of a woman wholly innocent of a crime being judged according to a law issued three centuries before. Frederick Charles Wace, magistrate and Mayor of Cambridge, took the central seat in the body of the courtroom. Wace was a fellow of St John's College, but he wasn't a man wedded to the ancient privileges of the university.

The new 'university wives', permitted since the 1880 change in the statutes, arrived from middle- and upper-middle-class families, from towns and counties with none of the social divisions of Cambridge. They came with fresh ideas and a desire to 'do good'. These well-connected women had an army of servants to run their homes and threw themselves into forming committees to alleviate the privations of the poor and heal the wounds of 'town and gown'. They wanted working-class women off the streets as much as Butler did but went about it in a kinder way – something socially and politically motivated women were doing all over the country.

The 'wives' set up training schools for servants. They organised health and welfare for mothers and babies. They achieved a great deal, and in doing so, began building bridges between the worlds of the town and the gown. Their husbands' heads were turned in ways that had been impossible a decade ago – talk at home and at dinner parties touched on the plight of the poor.

Thus, in the courtroom at the old castle, Frederick Wace had mixed feelings towards the case he was about to try. The townspeople prayed he would find a way to release Jane from the clutches of her oppressor; he wanted justice to prevail, whichever side it eventually fell. Despite her notoriety for drunken scuffles on the streets, this spirited 17-year-old was known as a 'likeable unfortunate'.

Seats in the sombre room had been snapped up. A handful of under-graduates slipped in too; the youthful temptation of being near a notorious young woman was worth the risk of a rebuke from a tutor. Their excitement was rewarded.

Jane Elsden, in clean clothes, was escorted from the cells to take a seat on one of the benches at the front of the courtroom. She was angry. She was ready to have her say, eager to expose the nasty system persecuting her freedom to roam as she pleased.

The first witness called was Agnes Grey, under matron from the Spinning House. 'The prisoner was discharged from the Spinning House on Tuesday last, after serving fourteen days …' she started, but Jane cut her off.

'… and I was took up again on Wednesday night!'

Agnes pressed on. 'She complained of a headache. I took her down-stairs to the yard and went to post a letter. On my return, in about ten minutes, I found the prisoner gone. The curtains in the chaplain's room had been pulled down.'

Jane could not passively sit still and listen. After all, this was 'her' trial. 'Anyone could get out; the door is never locked.' Anger and vengeance flowed out of her. 'Was not both doors open, Matron? No, they were both shut, but not locked,' she taunted. 'There is a door here and a door there, and you could have got through them and got out of the window into the street the same as I did. And …' she paused to emphasise the fact, 'I untied the blind. I did not pull it down.'

Her torrent of hot words triggered laughter in the courtroom, and delighted with such an appreciative audience, Jane paused only for a moment to glow in her success before continuing, 'Anybody would be glad to get out of that place. I have been to prison for six weeks, and I would rather do it all again than go into the Spinning House for a fortnight. I have always told Matron I would rather be in the town prison. You are kept warm and comfortable in that prison; it is more than you are there.' Then she loudly reminded everyone, 'I was not with any university men at all. No. I've broken no laws.'

Mr Balls, assigned to represent Jane, drew the court's attention to the Prisons Act of 1877, which passed control of prisons to the Home Office. This, he argued, surely stripped the vice chancellor of his prison and authority to issue sentences. 'This young woman,' Balls went on, 'was arrested and tried for an offence not known by any court in the land and sent to a prison whose legitimacy is uncertain.'

A warm feeling spread through Jane's tense body. She wanted to shout out in agreement but thought better of it. Having someone speaking up for her rights was a new and happy feeling for a young woman used to fighting her cause alone. But Musgrave Francis was quick to spoil the moment.

'I have documents relating to *Kemp vs Neville* in 1860,' he said. 'They prove the Spinning House is an approved prison. They prove the vice chancellor has the authority to imprison women there.'

'The key question,' Wace interrupted, 'hinges on whether the university retains the legal power to arrest women for simply walking in the street.'

After much debate, it was decided the case should be heard by a higher authority. Luckily, the assize judge was expected in Cambridge for the Spring Session the following day. Assize courts were held in local county towns across the country four times a year and were heard by senior 'circuit' judges with greater powers than local magistrates.

'Can I have bail?' Jane piped up.

'It's not worth applying,' the mayor kindly told her. 'It is only one night. The trial is booked for tomorrow.'

The courtroom emptied onto the streets of Castle Hill. Surely a higher authority would find in favour of Jane? But the show was far from over.

The Norfolk circuit of the assize court, covering the shire towns of Buckingham, Bedford, Huntingdon, Cambridge, Suffolk and Norfolk, was taking that spring's circuit judge, 68-year-old Charles Edward Pollock, on his usual tour of county towns. As a senior representative of Her Majesty's Government, Pollock took up residence at the Master's Lodge at Trinity College while the court was in session.

Stepping off his train from Huntingdon, he was greeted by station officials before being escorted to a waiting carriage that would convey him to his lodgings. There, the master, fellows, mayor and town dignitaries ceremonially greeted him before attending a special reception in his honour, where they sipped on mulled port and bit into specially made sweet biscuits.

As was so often the case, a close family connection between the college and the Pollock family already existed. Pollock's father had been at Trinity, gaining the title of Senior Wrangler – he scored the highest overall mark in mathematics for his year in 1806 – before immersing himself in politics and law.

Pollock himself had decided to dispense with a university education. Under his father's instruction, he immersed himself in law and was called to the Bar in 1847.

It was eleven o'clock in the morning of Tuesday, 17 February, when a packed courtroom rose to acknowledge the arrival in court of Baron Pollock. This time, tutors had forbidden undergraduates to attend the proceedings. The light drizzle of a dank morning clung in the air. Damp, heavy clothing gave off a musty scent.

It was Jane's fourth court appearance in just under a month. While the circuit judge attended a special ceremonial service at Great St Mary's Church on the Market Square – to pray for guidance before embarking on his days of judgement in Cambridge – Jane and the solicitor allocated to her, Mr Livett, sat in a private room, deep in conversation about securing her release. There is no record of whether freshly laundered clothes had reached her for this important day, but it was an appearance characterised by her crisp silence in court. Livett had counselled her well.

The jury were sworn in. Most of the morning's proceedings repeated what had been said the day before. Jane pleaded not guilty to escaping jail. Livet argued that the Prisons Act of 1877 did away with the privileges of the vice chancellor's court at the Spinning House. 'Jane Elsden has committed no offence in common law,' he argued. 'Yet the prisoner has been persecuted from start to finish. She was arrested by men who appeared, from the evidence, to be playing the part of spies, acting in the character of Russian police.' He claimed, 'The poor girl got twenty-one days in fifteen minutes. She is the victim of persecution.'

Pollock called for evidence from the Elizabethan charter permitting the arrest of women 'suspected of evil'. The charter, and a translation of it, were promised for the following day. The court adjourned.

The next day, copies of the charter, in Latin and English, were handed to Pollock. The Latin translation provided a point of contention between purists. The word '*suspectas*', appearing in the original charter, referred to women 'sometimes suspected', thus, any woman arrested must have been 'previously suspected' by the proctors. In this case, it was agreed that Jane Elsden had been 'suspected before', as she'd been found in the company of a member of the university.

Things didn't look good for Jane, but Livett had a plan. Here was a story of untold injustice. A tale ripe for the picking for the national press. He stood tall to deliver a passionate plea to save his client and damn the tyrannical system of hounding innocent women. 'This poor woman in the dock, hardly a woman, a mere girl of 17 years has been the victim of a cruel jurisdiction. In a free England, she has been dogged and dragged through no less than four courts. She was caught in a trap upon mere suspicion and brought before a court not recognised by the usual law. Let the jury imagine themselves in this court, held in a private room with no one else admitted and the prisoner allowed no representation. Her liberty being tampered with, this poor girl, in an unguarded moment, found the door and a window open and walked out.' The appreciative sound of hilarity rippled through the room on this remark. 'This unfortunate girl had committed no offence of which they could find her guilty. It was lynch law. Under this law, no woman in Cambridge is safe.' Merriment met this comment.

'There is no satisfactory evidence that this girl committed a crime and the irregularity of her arrest and trial show she was not in legal custody. Because she was not in lawful custody, she cannot be accused of escape. I appeal to the jury to acquit this poor girl and protect the rights of women in Cambridge.'

Loud cries of 'Hear, hear!' rang around the courtroom. It was 11.35 a.m. The jury were directed to retire.

They returned at noon. The foreman of the jury stood erect.

'Do you have a verdict?' Pollack asked.

'We do.'

'How do you find the defendant?'

'Guilty of escaping custody. But we would like to add a rider …'

Pollock silenced him with a raised hand. 'If it is merely on general grounds, I cannot receive it.'

'It is the feeling of the jury that it should be expressed,' insisted the foreman.

'You will have plenty of opportunities for making it known; I can't receive it,' Pollock said. 'I find the prisoner guilty of escape and restore her to the custody from which she has escaped.'

At this moment, Jane Elsden's voice was finally heard in court. The words she uttered were not deemed printable by any respectable newspapers. But in the kerfuffle, the foreman of the jury took his chance. Rising to his feet and raising his voice to a rallying cry, he relayed every word of the rider. 'We find that the vice chancellor's court is in need of revision!' he shouted.

Loud and fearless applause spread around the courtroom. Contempt for the outdated powers of the university was not restricted to the jury.

Pollock could not help sharing his thoughts with the men of the jury. 'If the vice chancellor's court is an improper one, it could be swept away by legislation,' he said. 'Now the public are acquainted with the facts, I imagine Parliament will be asked to revise a power so capable of inflicting such hardship. Such powers conferred long ago are obviously out of date in the latter part of the nineteenth century.'

This was a view taken up by some very influential people. People and Parliament could no longer ignore the tyranny of the university.

16

SAVING JANE

The Liberal Member of Parliament for Northampton was infamously unconventional. He was a mischief maker; a man who enjoyed humiliating Conservative Members of the House.

Sixty-year-old Henry Labouchere had entered politics out of curiosity and a conviction that the House would benefit from his radical beliefs. A born showman, he drew the crowds like a magnet, and he turned out to be the perfect person to leap into the ring to free Jane Elsden.

A renowned gambling man, his time at Trinity College, Cambridge, was largely spent attending the racecourse at Newmarket, where his losses were legendary, amounting to £6,000. His bachelor's degree was withheld after an accusation of cheating.

Aged 21 and in need of amusement, he voyaged to South America where the family had business. To their dismay, their profligate son fell for a travelling circus performer, eagerly joining her troupe as the 'Bounding Buck of Babylon'. His showpiece was jumping over obstacles attired in pink tights with a ribbon round his head.

Politically, he was 'a vehement opponent of feminism' and fiercely homophobic. His strengthening of the laws against homosexuality resulted in the imprisonment of Oscar Wilde. Sodomy was already a crime, but the Labouchere Amendment criminalised any sexual activity between men.

He also waged war against the abuse of privilege and his prevailing political ambition was the removal of the ruling Conservative Party. Nothing gave him more pleasure than throwing awkward questions at his adversaries across the crowded floor of the House. When he learnt about the woes of Jane Elsden, he immediately spotted the mileage in the case. He could turn the Elsden story to his advantage.

Almost daily, columns of newspaper print echoed the cries of people up and down the country demanding the university cease its tyrannical rule over the people of Cambridge. Yet one man remained glaringly silent on the matter. The Conservative Member for Cambridge, Mr Penrose Fitzgerald, had, it appeared, been struck dumb. Henry Labouchere presumed the silence stemmed from fear of offending the vice chancellor.

Penrose Fitzgerald had been educated at Cambridge, but unlike Henry Labouchere, had thrown himself into university life, having the honour of rowing in the Oxford and Cambridge Boat Race for two consecutive years. Perhaps Labouchere was right about his reluctance.

No word was heard either from Cecil Raikes, the university's Conservative Member of Parliament.[*]

The House of Commons had been dull for weeks. Few had braved the weather to sit through the dreary debates tabled so far that year. But on Friday, 20 February, two days after Jane's return to the Spinning House, a great number of MPs pushed through the yellow fog of London to ensure a seat in the House. The unpredictable Member for Northampton had tabled a question on 'University jurisdiction'. The House had a treat in store.

Silence fell as Labouchere rose to address the assembled members. Standing tall, with one hand casually thrust into a pocket and a half-smile itching to break over his bearded face, he turned his body to face the crowded chamber. For a brief moment, the only sound was of creaking oak as MPs shuffled to find comfort in their seats, preparing to devote to this man their full attention.

The question was judged not only to embarrass the absent borough MP from Cambridge, but also to take a swipe at Mr Matthews, the Home Secretary and a former lawyer, whose success at the Bar had not translated to the Commons. It was said his elevation to Home Secretary had been at the request of the queen, who had been impressed with his dealings in a celebrated divorce hearing. Yet he was known for 'always being a day behind everybody else'. It quickly became apparent he wasn't up to the job during the Jack the Ripper atrocities, when newspapers dubbed him 'never at home Matthews'. When trouble loomed, the Home Secretary was never to be found.

'Was the Home Secretary aware of the situation in Cambridge?' Labouchere enquired.

---

[*] Cambridge University elected its own member to the House, between 1603–1950.

'I have seen a newspaper report of the case in question,' Mr Matthews confirmed.

'Would he,' the MP wanted to know, 'consider the expediency of bringing a Bill to put an end to the jurisdiction of the vice chancellor over the inhabitants of Cambridge who are not members of the university?'

Matthews started his defence of the ancient law. 'The Jurisdiction of the vice chancellor's court has been reviewed …'

But Labouchere cut him off, knowing the Home Secretary was referring to the case of *Kemp vs Neville*. 'I don't care one sixpence about that,' Labouchere declared. 'What I ask is whether it is right and proper that the trial of any person should be conducted in private with nobody present but the vice chancellor and a couple of Bulldogs?'

The Home Secretary believed the Spinning House was a 'lawfully constituted court' and it was not his 'duty' to enquire further into the matter.

'Has he not heard of the Cass case?' Labouchere audibly threw the mocking remark over his shoulder as he eased himself back into seat.

The Home Secretary was unlikely to have forgotten the Cass case. Queen Victoria had asked him for the full details of the infamous incident that had occurred on the night of 28 June 1887. It is a case that draws fascinating parallels with what was happening on the streets of Cambridge.

A young servant girl called Elizabeth Cass was arrested in Regent Street, London, and accused of soliciting. On hearing the news, her employer rushed to her aid, explaining she had sent the girl on an errand to purchase gloves. At Elizabeth's trial the following day, the magistrate discharged her, but made it clear he didn't believe in her innocence, observing that no respectable woman should be walking in Regent Street at 9 p.m.

Her employer was incensed by the implication that she had committed perjury. She complained to the Metropolitan Police. Questions were asked in the House of Commons, followed by a debate on the case. The public wanted to know if the policeman was justified in arresting Miss Cass or whether he had made a mistake.

The Cass case confirmed fears that the Metropolitan Police abused their powers and arrested women without proper evidence. At the inquiry into what happened, the police were exposed as going to any lengths to blacken Elizabeth's character – they had produced a witness who turned out to have several aliases and under cross-examination, her language proved so offensive she was asked to leave the room. As a result of the inquiry, constables refused to arrest a prostitute unless absolutely compelled to do, such was their fear of making a mistake.

Like Elizabeth Cass, Jane became a symbol, a martyr to the cause of freedom. Her words, 'I thought I lived in a free England', echoed in the ears of many.

Correspondents to the *Cambridge Independent* newspaper were keen to ask questions about their own MP. 'Why do the people of Cambridge have to thank the representative of another constituency for calling the attention of Parliament in the case of Jane Elsden? What is our member doing? Here is a matter upon which the whole town is agreed, and yet the town member is dumb!'

The day after the Labouchere question, an urgent letter landed on the Home Secretary's desk. It was from Colonel Baker, Director of the Prison Gate Brigade of the Salvation Army. He wrote to say, 'The way her arrest was brought about was most discreditable.' He went on to emphasise that she had not accosted anyone or behaved in a disorderly manner and yet had been dragged through three courts. He suggested Jane be handed over to his own organisation, where Mrs Bramwell Booth would accommodate her in one of her new homes. There she would be encouraged to lead a better life.

The Salvation Army had made the connection between economic hardship and crime and offered practical solutions and rehabilitation through their Social Reform programmes. They 'saved' a great number of women who were prepared to live lives of prayerful obedience.

The following day's newspapers revealed that a 'philanthropic lady of title' had been in touch with Colonel Baker. She had offered to bring Jane to London and deliver her into the hands of the Salvation Army. It would have been impossible for the Home Secretary to ignore the involvement of such an esteemed lady of title.

Lady Lucy Lyttleton had married Liberal politician Lord Frederick Cavendish in 1864. The childless couple shared a passion for the education of women and girls. They were both heavily involved in furthering educational institutions in Yorkshire. In 1882, Cavendish was appointed Chief Secretary for Ireland, but tragedy struck on his first official visit to Dublin. On 8 May, he was walking in a park with a colleague when they were suddenly attacked, both dying of stab wounds. The heartrending event became known as the Phoenix Park Massacre.

His grieving widow declared she would devote her life to 'working for good'. Her pioneering work in women's education soon gained her great respect. She turned down an invitation to become Mistress of Girton College, Cambridge, to continue the spread of her work unhindered.

With such strong connections to Cambridge (her husband and brothers attended university there), she was able to intervene in the Jane Elsden case.

Meanwhile, as she continued to create headline news, a seething Jane Elsden settled back into life inside the unwelcoming walls of the Spinning House. Two weeks of boredom, cold and damp stretched before her. So, it was a welcome surprise when the matron sent Agnes to fetch Jane to one of the small rooms beyond the main prison block. There, Jane was instructed to sit as a small of party of neatly dressed women questioned her.

'Would you like to live a different life?' one of the ladies asked her.

Jane weighed up the ladies sitting before her, she didn't dislike them. 'I might,' she heard herself say.

'Would you like to go to London?'

Jane's eyes widened. 'I think …' she stumbled, not really understanding what was being said to her.

'You are a very fortunate young woman,' one of the ladies told her. A new life awaited Jane if she could embrace a righteous life.

Jane was desperate to be free.

'I could take you tomorrow,' the same lady informed her.

Jane had already lost all there was to lose. 'I'll come,' she said.

The next day, a female officer from the Salvation Army arrived to escort her to London where, under the guidance of the Women's Social Work Section, Jane's new life began. But could Jane be saved?

Snowflakes were falling on the morning of Tuesday, 24 February, as Jane climbed up the six steps leading to the front door of 259 Mare Street, Hackney, London. Behind her were sounds of shouting voices and horses' hooves clipping along the cobblestones. In front of her was a four-storey building. This was the Salvation Army Receiving Home for fallen women, also known as 'Rescue Headquarters'. Its door regularly swung open to embrace repentant young women.

Jane must have dug deep to find the courage to still her instinct to run. London was an exciting place for girls visiting from county towns. The capital was full of an energy that Cambridge lacked. Could Jane really turn her back on temptation?

The house at 259 Mere Street accommodated the Salvation Army's Department for Women's Social Work. This new initiative had been founded in 1887 to offer practical help. All too often, those saved on a Sunday had little choice but to return to houses of sin for the rest of the week. Mrs Bramwell-Booth had noticed this and had thrown herself behind the cause of more lasting salvation for such young women and girls.

Generally, the Salvation Army found posts for its charges as domestic servants. Yet not all were suited to such work and the organisation had pondered on what to do with such cases. Jane was about to find out the conclusion they had come to.

Inside No. 259, a slightly nervous Jane carefully studied the faces of the women around her. She detected kindness in their eyes, yet their stern, dark uniforms made Jane check her naturally abrasive nature. Captain Taylor carried out the verbal assessment. 'Are your parents alive?'

Jane gave her parents' names, address and her father's employment.

'Have you been to Sunday school?'

'Have you been to Salvation Army meetings?'

Jane had to confess that she had not attended Sunday school nor been to any such meetings. Details of Jane's life had been communicated from some unknown authority prior to her arrival. In her report, Captain Taylor noted that their new arrival had 'fallen' two years ago and was 'given to drink'. Her behaviour in Cambridge was described as 'very depraved naturally', but she was a fit and healthy young woman who was not, nor had ever been, 'diseased'.

Mrs Bramwell-Booth had worked out that some girls were not suited to the laborious kitchen drudgery required of a 'maid of all work'. It wasn't that they 'self-handicapped themselves in their struggle to make a living' by turning to sin, but a natural frailty made it difficult to cope with hard labour. She agreed that some girls might have a constitutional weakness towards immorality that was greatly accelerated by the impoverished lives they had led. Jane Elsden most likely fitted the latter classification.

The temptation of drink was frequently listed as the cause of a girl's downfall. But whatever condition girls arrived in, a great deal of trouble was taken to inspire them with hope: hope of betterment; hope they would rejoice in God and hope they would inspire others – the girls were 'saved to save others'.

Jane was sent to work as a book folder at Trade Headquarters in Clerkenwell. This modern printing business advertised itself as being 'one of the industrial branches of the Women's Social Wing'. She lived at the Salvation Army's Almeida Street Home, a short walk from the factory and where the other girls who were similarly employed lived.

Trade Headquarters offered the very best in working conditions and pay. The workers received 13s per week, with a small charge for board and lodging, comparing favourably with similar workers in Glasgow, printing Bibles and prayer books, whose pay was only 4 or 5s a week.

The Clerkenwell folding room boasted large windows which let in warm rays of sunlight that would play around the high ceilings, caressing the bent gold and brown heads as their ink-smudged fingers carefully twisted and turned the printed pages with the help of a folding stick. Each girl needed good eyesight and nimble fingers to ensure accurate folding. Each page must register with the other, the numbered corner being the gauging point. Once the sheets were folded, they passed to the stitcher.

Modern electric light dispersed the evening darkness or brightened the all-too-common days when dense yellow fog conquered daylight. Nothing halted the careful folding of the words of the Christian soldiers. This was better than being inside any prison – but Labouchere was right when he said in the House of Commons that Jane Elsden was not actually 'free'.

The organisation gave a dark dress and crisp white apron to each of the girls to be worn at work. They were urged to neatness – neat hair, neat, clean aprons and well-polished shoes. As Jane sat before her never-ending piles of pages, she must have felt an invisible, but always present, tension within her. She was in a room full of characters who could fly into a rage at the slightest provocation.

From childhood, Jane was permanently primed to defend herself against any slight. A great deal of tact and patience was needed from the female staff managing the girls. Quarrels were never far away from girls familiar with a volatile lifestyle. Jane's eventual discharge report makes it clear that Jane found it hard to conform. She was described as being 'quarrelsome by nature and troublesome to manage at times with a very quick and vengeful temper'.

Yet, every effort was made to make the girls feel at home. A small corner of the room was partitioned off to create a snug, homely dining room where the girls ate their regular meals. Dinner and tea were prepared and served by one of the girls from the Almeida Street home. Ten minutes of prayer preceded the one-hour dinner break at 12.30 and visitors who came to admire the industrious workers would often lead the dinnertime prayers. Half an hour was assigned for an afternoon tea break – and more devotions. A working day of folding pages that began at 8.30 finished at 7 in the evening. Order and obedience were vital.

The cause saved the lives of hundreds of girls, according to the Salvation Army newsletter, *The Deliverer*, which told many tales of young women whose lives were 'saved'. But Jane's story would not appear in those pages. Given her track record, it is astonishing the feisty Jane lasted more than a week. The tolerance and kindness of the staff must have been endlessly tried, but persistent insubordination was not tolerated. To the surprise of those who knew her, Jane Elsden endured just over three months of care and prayer, but as Mrs Bramwell-Booth used to say, drink always preceded ruin.

After receiving her quarterly pay, Jane popped out for a glass of beer. One drink led to another. Soon Jane didn't care what trouble awaited her on her return home. Nor did she care for anyone caring to reprimand her for her drunkenness.

That evening, Jane returned to Almeida Street for the last time. It was concluded that Jane Elsden was 'naturally very wild and wicked'. Although her discharge papers did note that 'at times she manifested a strong affection and was often genuinely grateful to all the officers who tried to help her'.

By the end of June 1891, Jane Elsden was back in Cambridge where she resumed her drunken life on its streets. The return of a girl hailed as a martyr to the cause of freedom should have been accompanied by fanfares, but memories of her escapades were fading. In its place, the old town and gown quarrels had resumed, but this time the town was led by a mayor who was determined to promote a new order.

17

UNDER PRESSURE

As Jane Elsden laboured away inside the Salvation Army's book-binding factory in Clerkenwell, opposition to the powers of the proctors was gaining momentum. Only a few miles away from where she sat skilfully twisting her folding stick, her name was being mentioned at a meeting of the South Kensington Women's Liberal Association.

That day in March 1891, the women were debating the 'special powers' held by the proctors in Cambridge. It was agreed they would write to the Mayor of Cambridge, calling for the end of university jurisdiction.

Jane Elsden would not know that at the same time as the Women's Liberal Association were about to demand an end to the power of the university, so too were the ratepayers of Cambridge. Henry Labouchere was following events too, delighted at the discord he had sown. He was pleased to hear that the town's disgraced MP, Mr Penrose Fitzgerald, had been barred from attending public meetings. With her arrest and imprisonment causing heated national debate, surely the special powers granted to the university four centuries ago would not survive into another?

On a wet Monday morning in the first week of April, thirty-two members of the borough council filed into the wood-panelled chamber at the Town Hall on the Market Square in Cambridge. A single item stood on the special agenda: 'university jurisdiction'.

Frederick Charles Wace, mayor and graduate of St John's College, embodied a new order of men who wanted to bring harmony to the town. First at the meeting, that drizzly April morning when daylight only shyly peered through the windows of the council chamber, the mayor read out the letter he'd received from the Women's Liberal Association in South Kensington. 'It stated,' he said, 'their disapproval of the "special powers" conferred upon the authorities of Cambridge to arrest and inflict "summary punishment" on persons other than members of the university.'

The letter was not favourably received. The thirty-two councillors unanimously agreed that outsiders had no right to address the council on such a question. The 'interfering' letter was rejected. So, too, was an unsigned petition from local parish clergy stating their fears for the moral virtue of the town without the continued attention of the proctors and their men.

A warning came also in the pages of the *Cambridge Chronicle*, whose editor alerted its readers to the potential financial losses to the town if an Act were obtained to do away with proctorial authority. The newspaper, read mainly by those siding with the university in any matter, underlined the 'financial contribution an additional three thousand and five hundred inhabitants made to the town's population', albeit for only 'twenty-four weeks a year'. Each student, the newspaper pointed out, spent approximately £200 a year in the town. Parents would hesitate in sending their sons to Cambridge if there were not proper measures for maintaining moral authority, the paper warned.

The hero of the hour at the meeting turned out to be Councillor George Bullock who, it was acknowledged a few months later in his obituary, 'had worked his whole time to serve his fellow townsmen', a possible reason for his untimely death aged only 56. He was a man greatly respected for his fair-mindedness in his role on the Board of Guardians at the workhouse in Mill Road, Cambridge, and his steadfastness in supporting the ratepayers of Cambridge. This esteemed townsman treated the chamber to a short history of town and gown relations.

'The privileges of the university were conferred in the reign of Elizabeth I – a time of absolute monarchy,' he declared. 'There has been unbroken revolt against these rules by the townspeople since the very time they were made.

'We may as well go back to the Book of Moses if we are to take ancient history as our guide,' he teased. 'We live in a more enlightened era. Is it right that the town still be governed by privileges handed down from a different age?'

Bullock concluded his speech by declaring his intention to vote for an Act of Parliament to remove the powers of the university. Shouts of 'Hear, hear!' rang out.

But Councillor Kenney counselled caution. He was keen to shield innocent undergraduates from temptation. 'The smallness of Cambridge makes it impossible for the ordinary law to apply,' he warned. 'If nothing but the common law prevailed in Cambridge, given its closeness to London, I fear we would soon be swarming with persons of bad character.'

'The problem lies with undergraduates' behaviour,' a councillor chipped in. 'Only a few weeks ago some undergraduates were seen pestering girls as they left church in a nearby village. The vicar invited the proctors to visit and discipline the men. The problem went away.'

'No respectable young lady can walk from the railway station to Trinity College without being grossly insulted by junior members of the university,' said another.

'In many cases, the university men are the great disturbers of the public peace,' someone piped up. 'I've seen them. They link arms and sweep the pavements clear, I have seen, over and over again, respectable females insulted by them. They loll out of windows, drink their grog, and throw oranges about. The proctors should be policing their behaviour.'

The story chimed with Bullock, who said out loud what was on the mind of most. 'The university authorities should deal with their own members, and the town authorities should deal with the inhabitants of the town.'

'These women need our sympathy,' another said, quickly adding, 'I do not defend prostitution' – for anyone daring to defend the young women walking the streets was instantly branded by the opposition as being a supporter of immoral behaviour.

It was pointed out that the greatest obstacle standing in the way of an immediate Act of Parliament was that it could be a lengthy process. But the mayor wanted action, not delay. 'Without the likelihood of a hearing in the House until next spring, a dual course of action is needed to secure the reforms. We will need …' A short sigh escaped from his lips as he exhaled the deep breath he'd just taken. 'We will need the borough MP to help us secure an Act.'

Penrose Fitzgerald, MP for Cambridge, was the right man to approach for advice on the promotion of a Bill. But the town were still angry at him for dodging his duty to the townspeople who had elected him. Yet he knew the time had come for the university to moderate its powers over the town. Both he and Cecil Raikes, MP for Cambridge University, advised the vice chancellor that the matter was 'extremely delicate'. Feelings were running high in both camps.

The meeting in the council chamber concluded with an agreement that the mayor would write to the vice chancellor demanding he overturn the proctors' powers to arrest women and leave it to the police to keep the streets 'clean'. In the meantime, the council would set to work on a petition for an Act of Parliament to overthrow the ancient law allowing the arrest and imprisonment of women suspected of 'evil'.

In the summer months, the oozing mud that usually sloshed around the streets of Cambridge dried to a crumbling pale hardness – the perfect texture to powder the air with clouds of dust as the clattering hooves of horses pulling all manner of carts and carriages pounded the dry roads. They were mostly retired Newmarket racehorses and sometimes students were tempted to 'race' them along the streets. But the clamour of the streets was unheard in the cool and quiet of Trinity College, where Montague Butler was still wrangling over the demands set out in the letter from the mayor, wishing he hadn't ordered the rearrest of Jane Elsden.

Given the fact that the feminist campaigner Josephine Butler was his sister-in-law, he was well aware of her views on the situation in Cambridge. She had denounced the Contagious Diseases Acts of the 1860s. Now a widow in her sixties, her campaigning zeal had not diminished. Although there is no evidence that the women forced into the Spinning House were routinely inspected for 'disease', Josephine Butler was vocal in her rage at the treatment of women suspected of prostitution in the garrison towns. In her essay 'The Constitution Violated', penned in 1871, she wrote that the 'malicious whisper of a single man … may destroy the character of a woman' – which had happened to Emma Kemp in 1860, and was the fear of every woman who walked in the streets of Cambridge after dark without a chaperone. She was shocked at the injustice of the Contagious Diseases Acts, where 'any woman found associating, under any circumstances, with a man, who cannot produce a certificate of her marriage with him, was to be labelled a prostitute'. Her thoughts on 'proctorial authority' in Cambridge and the Spinning House were shared with her brother-in-law. They were hard to ignore. So was the role Lady Lyttleton had played in Jane Elsden's release.

So, it was perhaps not a great surprise when, in June 1891, a narrow oblong of newsprint appeared in the Cambridge newspapers announcing that six cells inside the Spinning House were to be refashioned to create a courtroom for the public to enter to witness future trials. The cost of the undertaking, it was reported, would be £160. Something or someone had finally persuaded the vice chancellor that the proctorial system needed modifying.

It was early in July when the mayor finally received an official reply to his letter:

The Council of the Senate have made certain modifications in the method of procedure adopted at future Spinning House trials. In future the trials will be open to the public, all evidence in future will be heard on oath and the prisoner permitted legal assistance.

The Senate had realised it was essential they kept ahead of outside interference that could deprive them of their powers. Delaying was no longer an option.

In agreeing to these new measures, the university retained the power to arrest women suspected of 'evil', something the police were not empowered to do – they needed evidence before detaining a woman on a charge of soliciting. Only the ancient Elizabethan charter guarded that privilege, and the university would cling by their very fingertips to that right.

The memory of Jane Elsden's daring escape began to fade, but she would secure herself a place in the history of Cambridge. Her brazen defiance had forced the university to modify its tyrannical regime. In doing so, she paved the way for greater change. The town and gown were now poised to see what would happen the next time a girl was arrested. They didn't need to wait long.

A RURAL LIVING

It was late spring in 1877 when Inspector John Jacobs of the City of Ely Police Force tethered his horse at the home of the Hopkins family in the Fenland village of Sutton. In one hand, he clutched a warrant he had been instructed to serve that day. His other hand was balled into a fist, ready to hammer hard on the front door of the modest cottage in Red Lion Lane.

At his first knock, he sensed stirring in an upstairs room, but no one came to unlatch the door. He mulled over returning to Ely. However, his orders were to press the warrant into the hands of the accused that day. His second volley of hard thuds roused the complaining sound of a crying infant. It was cry that could not be ignored.

A few days before the inspector's visit, Sergeant Pryor, a soldier in the 4th Suffolk Regiment, had reacted with outrage when his wife objected to his 'regular intimacy' with Alice, the eldest of the three Hopkins daughters – the third-born of the nine Hopkins children squeezed into the cottage in Red Lion Lane. He frequently retired to the bedroom of the 21-year-old when he wasn't on parade.

Threats and blows had rained down on Mrs Pryor, who took her bruised body to Ely Police Station to press charges for assault. Taking pity on the young wife, a magistrate issued a warrant binding Sergeant Pryor to keep the peace. It was Inspector Jacobs' duty to serve that notice, and when he discovered the officer was not at home, he was helpfully directed to the lane where the Hopkinses dwelt.

The crying child couldn't disguise that someone was probably at home. The keen ears of the inspector detected the sound of a latch. The door creaked ajar. Mrs Hopkins stood on the threshold. Her bristling, bawdy reputation went before her, Jacobs braced himself.

'You've woke my Daisy!' The sound of her voice mimicked the deep scowl on her face.

'Is Sergeant Pryor here?' enquired the inspector.

'What business is it of yours?' Mrs Hopkins parried.

'I've a warrant to serve.'

Heavy reluctant footsteps were heard descending the staircase while Mrs Hopkins stood guard with a damp-eyed child firmly pressed to her bosom.

'You may as well open the door,' came the angry words of a man in army breeches.

Reluctantly, Mrs Hopkins swung the door wider but remained an unmovable fixture as Jacobs pressed the unwelcome document into Pryor's hands.

Over a decade later, that small child's name would be mentioned in newspapers in London and New York. For it was Daisy Hopkins whose arrest and imprisonment in the Spinning House ignited the final bitter showdown between town and gown. She would be the first woman to be tried in the new courtroom inside the Spinning House. The first woman to have legal representation to challenge her arrest. The first where witnesses were sworn in, and the first whose case was open to the public. It was huge moment in the history of the town. A century later, Daisy Hopkins would still be spoken of by law lecturers and forever linked to the downfall of Cambridge University's private prison. But that spring day, all the young Daisy wanted was the soothing comfort of her mother's arms.

Soon after the inspector's visit, economic crisis came knocking on the Hopkinses door. The village of Sutton was becoming less and less the rural idyll of past times. Bad crops, bad prices and mechanisation were forcing agricultural workers off the land. The Fens had witnessed bloody riots over the introduction of machinery. Depression followed. Once famed for being the 'granary of England', farmers throughout East Anglia were in trouble. By 1879, earning an honest living toiling on the rich Fenland soil was becoming impossible for many. But the ever-resourceful Mrs Hopkins had a plan.

Two years after the inspector's visit, Henry Hopkins swapped rich black soil for beer as a means of making both ends meet. At his wife's suggestion, he became landlord of the Black Horse pub in Sutton High Street. However, once the harvest had been brought home in 1881, the family faced the fact that a publican's life was as precarious as that of an agricultural labourer.

Instead, Mrs Hopkins hatched the perfect plan. The family abandoned the barrels in the cellar of the Black Horse. The five elder boys scattered to coal fields far away in search of a living. Mr Hopkins loaded the family's possessions onto a cart and the horses lumbered their way to a house in Potters Lane, Ely.

The horse heaving the Hopkinses chattels drew up in Potters Lane, one of the humblest parts of the cathedral city of Ely. The narrow, winding lane that bordered the gasworks was close to the clatter of the railway station. Here was new ground for the delicate 7-year-old Daisy, and her 9-year-old brother, Charles, to explore, once their chores were done. And it was in Potters Lane that Mrs Hopkins, Alice, then aged 25, and Lydia, aged 16, were urged to find a way to pay the bills.

While Mr Hopkins bore a reputation for being a respectable, hard-working man, Mrs Hopkins boasted a different reputation. Not long after settling her crockery in the cupboards of her new home, neighbours whispered about being disturbed by the repeated knocking on Mrs Hopkins' door. 'Come in, come in!' she trilled to the gentlemen callers who, using the landmark of the Royal Oak public house on the corner of the slender lane, found their way to what was on offer at the Hopkins house.

Over the course of six years, spiteful gossip turned to complaints that reached the ears of the Reverend William Colville Wallis, Secretary of the Ely branch of the Society for the Protection of Public Morals. So often was he notified that the Hopkins family were a bad influence on the parish that he felt obliged to keep an eye on the comings and goings in Potters Lane. He himself witnessed undergraduates alighting from carriages of the Cambridge train; their destination being Potters Lane.

Further gossip had reached his ears. The youngest Hopkins daughter, Daisy, had already been encouraged to have 'connections with men'.

The Criminal Law Amendment Act of 1885 might just have rescued Daisy from her mother's enthusiasm to get her 'working'. Daisy would have been 12 years old around the time of the reverend's investigation. The Act, among other things, raised the age of consent from 13 to 16.

The change was demanded due to a series of shocking revelations. In the 1880s, a newspaper editor and advocate of social reform, W.T. Stead, wrote a series of articles in the *Pall Mall Gazette*. He proved that underage girls could be bought, or abducted, and forced into 'the white slave trade' for £5 – about £600 today. The article caused a sensation and the question of age of consent began appearing in a firm question.

In November 1886, Inspector John Jacobs dutifully paid his second official visit to a home inhabited by the Hopkins family. 'You're to quit,' he informed Mrs Hopkins.

'Why?' she demanded to know. She wasn't a woman to cower from anyone.

'Reverend Wallis,' Jacobs replied. 'There's been complaints.'

'No truth in them,' she informed him, as her mind battled against the impertinence of such people. 'You can't turn me out!' she shouted. 'I'll appeal.' And she did, buying herself six weeks to come up with a new plan.

During the first week in January 1887, the Hopkins family, minus a married Alice, arrived at 36 Gold Street, Cambridge, in the heart of Barnwell. Straight away, their new neighbours unpacked the morsels of scandal the family brought with them. What had the eldest two girls been up to in Ely? They wondered what the youngest daughter, the frail-looking 14-year-old Daisy Hopkins, recently apprenticed as a dressmaker, might already be up to. They weren't alone.

Henry Mason was a special constable employed by the university – a Bulldog, as they were commonly called. Not a day passed without him dutifully sniffing out tell-tale morsels of gossip about the true characters of the young women living in Barnwell. Since the national outrage about the high-handed powers of the university to arrest women, the proctors had instructed the Bulldogs to collect 'evidence' about the characters of the women they directed their masters to arrest. Mason sensed the need to observe the comings and goings of the Hopkins family. Rumour had reached his ears that the house in Gold Street was where Lydia 'entertained' callers. There were fears the younger sister, Daisy, would fall into the same business once she reached 16.

Mason wasn't the only person keeping an eye on the Hopkins family. Miss Elizabeth Rowley, an officer from the Salvation Army, had taken an

interest in the family. At first, she was relived to notice Daisy swelling the
rows of children watching magic lantern shows at the meetings of the
Barnwell Band of Hope, but when her name appeared on the Cambridge
Association for the Care of Girls list of girls who were living in a 'dangerous home', Rowley began to fear the worst.

'Have you found work?' she asked Daisy as soon as she left school.

''Prenticed to Mrs Lawson,' Daisy told Rowley. 'Learning dressmaking.'

For almost two years, Mason and Rowley noted her attendance at
Mrs Lawson's. But long hours spent folded over yards of seams didn't
suit Daisy's delicate constitution.

'There's a knife going through me,' wailed Daisy, one morning.

Mrs Hopkins didn't like the look of things. Daisy was plucking at her
bedsheets, twisting hard at the pain inside her. 'Fetch Doctor Rygate!'
commanded the worried mother.

Dr Rygate, who lived not too far away in Jesus Lane, arrived in haste
to examine the patient. He noted a distended stomach.

'Let me see your throat?' There, he detected several sores. Privately he
suspected a certain amount of hysteria in the patient. 'I'll mix a gargle.
Fetch it tomorrow,' he told Mrs Hopkins.

The daily spasms passed but didn't disappear and long hours of work
became impossible. Her needlework career came to a close. More medicine was required and the bills mounted.

Mrs Hopkins knew exactly how Daisy could earn 5s in no time at all.
Her 16th birthday was not far away and she'd heard talk of an elegant
woman called Jemima Watson. The lovely Jemima was a well-known
courtesan. Set up in fine, fashionable lodgings in the town, she regularly
entertained aristocratic members of the university. No one dared arrest
Jemima or shove her into the Spinning House. A plan began to take shape
in Mrs Hopkins' mind.

Mason soon noticed the change in Daisy's routine. He was worried. He
spoke to Miss Hannah Elsden, Matron of the Cambridge Female Mission.
'Has Daisy Hopkins come under your notice?' he enquired.

'She has,' Miss Elsden said.

'Has she fallen?' Mason asked.

'I've seen her. All dressed up in fine clothes.' Miss Elsden confirmed
the worse. 'Being paraded up and down Maids Causeway by her mother.'

Next, Mason spoke to Miss Elizabeth Rowley from the Salvation
Army. 'Has Daisy Hopkins come under your notice?' he asked.

'She has,' she confirmed. 'The mother came to a concert at the hall. I asked her why she didn't put a stop to Lydia and Daisy's behaviour. "Oh, I encourage every wickedness," she laughingly informed me.'

The evidence against Daisy Hopkins was mounting in Mason's mind. So, he consulted Police Constable Naylor, who beat the streets of Barnwell.

Naylor had information to share. 'I was called to Mrs Bell's house in Sun Street last week,' he said. 'Some boys were throwing stones up at a window. Someone complained about the commotion. Daisy Hopkins was in there.'

Mason wanted every detail.

'The boys tied up the door. They wanted to make sure the people inside couldn't get out.'

'What time of day was this?' asked Mason.

'About four o'clock in the afternoon. Market day, it was,' Naylor remembered. On market day, Cambridge filled with farmers. Once their pocketbooks bulged with profit, it was time for pleasure.

Naylor continued with his story. 'I untied the door and on the other side was an old farmer and Daisy Hopkins. "You should be ashamed of yourself to be found in such a place," I told the man. Daisy claimed she was collecting laundry from Mrs Bell. I said to her, "Where do you get the money for such fine clothes?"'

'My fiancé, Frederick Robinson, he likes me to dress well,' she told him. 'He is a professional gentleman,' she boasted.

Robinson was a French polisher living in the nearby village of Newnham. Was Mrs Hopkins' plan of setting her daughter up in splendour coming to fruition?

Ever the diligent sleuth, Mason questioned Caroline Bell, who knew the Hopkins family well.

'Robinson knocks her about,' she told Mason. 'He's got the key to Daisy's brother's house at 10 Gold Street. He expects Daisy to be there for him. I've often been sent to fetch her for Robinson. He gets cross if she's not there when he comes to see her.'

Mason never found out that when visiting London, Robinson would telegraph his fiancée, commanding her to join him in his lodgings, telling her to get a late train, a slow and cheap option that would deliver his fiancée early the following morning.

One evening, after a weary Daisy had waited over an hour for Robinson to arrive at her house, she went out to look for him. On seeing

Police Constable Wright, who lived near Gold Street, she asked, 'You seen Mr Robinson? He promised to come to my house?'

'Not seen him today,' the constable replied.

'I waited in for him. He hasn't come.'

Constable Wright couldn't help but make note of the fresh bruising encircling one of Daisy's eyes.

'We had a quarrel last night,' she confessed.

'Let him wait,' she declared. 'When the boys come up with the mortar boards, I will have a nice boy. Not one to knock me about.'

It was October 1891 and Daisy's search for a 'nice boy' began in earnest. And from that moment, Daisy Hopkins' liberty was in peril.

Mason did his duty. Her name was placed on the list of women to be arrested if found on the streets of Cambridge. PC Naylor recommended Daisy's name be added to the police's list of known prostitutes. She might not have known it, but from that moment, the proctor and his men were eager for her to put a foot wrong.

19

THE ARREST

A Fenland fog was spreading its cold, misty fingers through the town on the night of Wednesday, 2 December, as the proctor and his men turned into Pembroke Street. In the distance, a clock struck the half-hour. In thirty minutes, the bells of several churches and chapels would chime eleven, relieving the men of their night-time duties.

The trio had started their patrol on the streets closest to the riverbank, where most of the colleges stood. But now they turned onto the slightly higher ground of Botolph Lane, making their way towards Pembroke Street and then, they anticipated, towards Emmanuel College. Suddenly, a shrill cry pierced the stillness. Immediately looking around for the culprit, they saw the outline of a woman sheltering in the shadow of a nearby doorway.

'What are you doing?' the proctor, Reverend Frederick Wallis, wanted to know.

'Sorry, Sir, just shouting to a friend,' came the reply.

Wallis thought he recognised the woman's face. He thought he'd arrested her before but couldn't recall her name. The following year, he would describe her as being 'half drunk and of a bad character' when asked to describe the events of that night.

'What is your name?'

'Cook,' she replied. Laura Cooper had no intention of revealing her real name.

'Well, stop loitering about. Get home, or you will be in trouble,' he warned.

Meanwhile, guessing the cry had been delivered to warn someone close by, the Bulldogs, Alfred Kirby and Henry Mason, edged their way along Tennis Court Road, a nearby ill-lit street. Hugging the shadows cast by the high walls of Downing College, Kirby and Mason crept forward until the meagre light from the broadly spaced gaslights revealed the outline of a young man and woman deep in conversation.

As they neared the couple, they debated, then agreed, that the young woman might be Daisy Hopkins; thanks to Mason, her name was on the list of women to be 'brought in' if found on the streets after dark. But caution was everything. Everyone was still jittery following the arrest and very public trials of Jane Elsden earlier that year. During his last remaining months as vice chancellor, Butler had agreed that in future, women sent to the Spinning House would have legal assistance, with witnesses sworn in before giving testimony. A new courtroom had been created inside the Spinning House, its freshly whitewashed walls and wooden benches stood ready and waiting.

In October 1891, the broadminded, statesmanlike John Piele was installed as vice chancellor. In truth, the forward-thinking Piele, Master of Christ's College, arrived in his new post already uneasy about the changes his predecessor, Montague Butler, had made to the Spinning House. He'd already debated the thorny inconsistencies of being judge and jury in the new courtroom with his father-in-law, attorney William Kitchener. Thus, one of his first actions was to consult London solicitors Wright & Scott to help him understand his powers. He questioned his right to call for an adjournment, remand or grant bail in this new court. Could he still deliver justice while adhering to rules laid out in the ancient charter and operating within the law of the land? It was a complex situation; something Butler had not thought through. And Wright & Scott were struggling to come up with an answer.

As Kirby and Mason continued their vigilant progress along Tennis Court Road, they noticed the man talking to the girl wasn't wearing academicals: neither a cap nor gown. But Mason, on getting close enough to hear the man's voice, thought he recognised him as an undergraduate from Jesus College. They weighed up the situation. On balance, they were certain it was Daisy Hopkins but, as the man was not dressed according to university regulations, it was possible she didn't know he was a member of the university.

'Want me?' asked a startled Daisy as the men approached.

'What are you doing?' asked Kirby.

Exactly what Daisy Hopkins was doing on that evening can only be guessed at as she never had the chance to be correctly questioned on the matter. But she didn't miss a beat in telling Kirby, 'Showing him the way.'

Thrown off guard by her unruffled response, the Bulldogs erred on the side of caution. They knew a miscalculation could rouse bitter unrest between town and gown.

'You can go,' Kirby told her.

'Can I go too?' asked the man.

'Sir, I believe you are a member of the university,' Kirby said, a certain haughtiness catching in his voice.

'No, Sir, I'm not,' claimed the man.

'I recall visiting your rooms last term to collect a fine,' Mason said. 'You were fined for smoking on an omnibus whilst wearing academic dress.' The fine had been for 6s 6d and was duly paid.

The undergraduate fumbled in his pockets. 'Take this!' He pushed a sovereign into Kirby's hand. 'Let's forget about it.' He already faced a fine for being 'incorrectly dressed' and he didn't relish the additional trouble of being found in the company of a young woman from the town.

'I will not!' spat Kirby, a man already rich in his own importance and contempt for those abusing the rules of the university.

The undergraduate, noticing the proctor was nearing, desperately tried to push a further 5s into Kirby's hand.

As many undergraduates had annual incomes of £200 plus, and the Bulldogs £50 a year, turning a blind eye was tempting, but not for a man like Kirby. 'No Sir. The proctor will deal with this,' Kirby confirmed.

Within minutes, Wallis had arrived to take charge.

'We found Daisy Hopkins talking to this man,' Kirby reported.

'Name?' Wallis demanded.

'Charles Russell. But I ...'

'College?' The proctor only wanted facts.

'Jesus. Sir, I ...'

'Return to your rooms. I'll speak to your tutor later.'

Wallis turned his attention to Kirby and Mason. 'Where's the girl?'

'Sent her off, Sir,' Kirby replied.

'He wasn't in his academicals,' Mason explained.

'Bring her in,' Wallis demanded. 'Her name is on the list.' He was certain he had clear proof that an offence against the charter had taken place.

Kirby and Mason rushed off to find Daisy. It didn't take long. She was in the next street, Lensfield Road, where she stood chatting to a young man, Charles Camps, who lived in Barnwell. Both were astonished to see the Bulldogs. Only a short time ago, they'd told her she was free to go. But now, in their panic to follow orders, Daisy was thrust against some iron railings. The rough tussle tore the gathered shoulder seam of her dress as she was pinned back by her arms.

'Good God, what have I done?' she cried out.

'You were seen walking with a member of the university,' the proctor told her.

'I didn't know he was a gownsman! He wasn't wearing his cap and gown, how was I to know?' she shouted as she tried to escape. 'I was only showing him the way!'

She urged Charles Camps, 'Go quick, fetch my parents.'

'You're coming with us,' the proctor told her. And on his orders, Kirby and Mason grabbed her elbows, forcing her along the street. She knew where they were taking her, but she was determined not to go.

'I am not well, I have the quinsy,' she protested. The quinsy is a severe, inflamed infection of the throat which can be covered with whitish creamy secretions. 'I'm under the doctor,' Daisy pleaded. 'Tell them to take their dirty hands off me,' she insisted as the salt of the tears tumbling down her face stung at her sore throat.

'Don't touch her if she goes quietly,' Wallis commanded.

Mason whispered, 'You must go, and the more quietly you go the better it will be for you.'

'I've done nothing wrong!' Daisy wailed. 'I was only showing the man the way.' But taking Mason's wise advice, she abandoned her struggle.

As she was marched through the streets, tears rolling down her face, she cried out, 'Fetch my parents, please. I live at 36 Gold Street in Barnwell. Please, please someone help me!'

A small crowd gathered to enjoy the spectacle. Excited words spread that a girl had been arrested. If the girl was charged, the new courtroom would witness its first public trial. By the time the group reached the Spinning House, quite a throng of followers had collected. They watched the proctor pound the knocker on the Spinning House door.

The church bells announced the arrival of eleven o'clock. The freshly painted courtroom lay in complete darkness inside the prison. Would the townspeople finally get a chance to see it, they wondered?

Mrs Johnson, the ageing matron, had retired for the night, leaving the under matron, Agnes Grey, to wait up in case the proctor called. For months, all the pair had done was look after the prison while builders first quoted for then carried out the alterations to create the new courtroom ordered by Montague Butler. Since the national outcry about the arrest of Jane Elsden, arrests had plummeted to none, so worried were the proctor and his men about making a mistake. But Mason was a confident man.

The loud knock on the prison door made Agnes jump. As she scurried to open the door, she could hear a female voice shouting, 'Fetch my parents!' Daisy didn't stop appealing for help until the shock of finding herself in the inner courtyard of the Spinning House froze her vocal cords. This was where thousands of young women before her had waited. Each one unsure of their fate. It was here, in 1846, where Elizabeth Howe had trembled; in 1860, where Emma Kemp had tried to protect her young sister Louisa; where a complaining Jane Elsden had protested her innocence only ten months before.

Agnes beckoned the party to a small lime-washed room beyond the entrance hall, where she'd placed pen and ink and the latest Committal Book. It was the third of three weighty volumes recording the name, age, address, employment and parish of each girl and the names of their parents, if still living. Wallis carelessly scratched in the details of Daisy's arrest on the book's stiff cream paper, allocating her a new number – she had not been inside before:

Number 525 – Daisy Hopkins.
Age: 17.
Parish: St Andrew the Less.
Parents or friends: Henry Hopkins, father.
Last situation: Mrs Lawson, 10 Brunswick Walk.
Date of apprehension: 2 December 1891.
Present address: 36 Gold Street.
By whom apprehended: Frederic Wallis.

'What am I charged with?' Daisy asked.

'You are charged with walking with a member of the university.'

'I'm being attended by Dr Rygate for the quinsy, please send for him,' Daisy implored. 'You can't keep me here.'

'I'm afraid I can,' Wallis told her.

But mindful of the death of Elizabeth Howe, forty-five years before, Kirby was sent to speak to Dr Rygate. He urged that the Spinning House doctor be called if the vice chancellor didn't release the girl the following day.

Agnes took Daisy to Cell 10 on the ground floor. It contained a bed, but no fireplace. Opposite it was a large, antiquated stove, the same one that had been installed following the outcry about the damp conditions in the Spinning House back in 1860. It wasn't up to the task. Cold still penetrated every corner of the Spinning House.

'I'm so cold. I'm not well. My throat is sore,' Daisy told Agnes. 'Can I air the room and warm myself at the stove?'

The prison hadn't entertained an inmate for months. A musty damp clung in the air and on the bedding inside every cell. Agnes swung open the heavy door and placed a chair by the stove. 'Warm yourself.'

'Can I air the bedding?' Daisy asked.

Being told she could, Daisy pulled the sheets and blankets off the mattress and draped them close to the stove before huddling there herself.

While Daisy tended to her bedding, a breathless Charles Camp arrived in Gold Street. 'Come quick!' he panted to Mrs Hopkins. 'Daisy is inside the Spinning House.'

Like another mother, thirty-one years before, Mrs Hopkins rushed to the prison and hammered her fists on its locked doors. She waited. Nothing happened. She struck the doors again, crying out, 'Let me in! Let me in!'

She caught the proctor as he left the building. 'She is not well, Sir,' she pleaded. 'You can't put her in there. What's she done wrong?'

Wallis ignored her.

She persisted. 'She's under the doctor. You can't keep her in there!'

'She was found in the company of a member of the university,' came the sweeping dismissal.

Mrs Hopkins caught Agnes just as she was locking the door behind him. 'I need to see her,' she begged.

Agnes edged open the door, beckoning Mrs Hopkins forward. 'You can talk to her in the corridor,' she kindly offered. 'But only for a few minutes.'

Thirty minutes of tears and talk through a locked door at the end of the corridor leading to the cells was just long enough for Mrs Hopkins to hatch a plan. A version of the truth that would maintain Daisy's innocence through three separate trials, in three different towns.

It was midnight when Daisy finally faced her fate for that evening. 'Ring this.' Agnes handed her a small bell. 'I won't be far away.' She brought in a nightlight too, which provided a glimpse of warmth before Daisy heard a key turning in the lock of her cell door.

All was silent except for the rattle and thud of the heating system, but sleep was elusive. Daisy pulled the prison blankets around her small frame, trying to fill in the gaps that let in the cold. Fear began to paralyse her.

Agnes heard the bell ring at about two o'clock in the morning. 'I can't sleep!' wailed Daisy.

'Lie down and try.'

Several hours passed, the bell was rung again. 'Yes?' asked Agnes.

'I don't feel well. Can I have some water?'

'I'll fetch some.' Agnes filled a cup from the pump at the end of the corridor and unlocked the cell door.

It was the first time in her life Daisy had slept in an empty place. In her mind, all she could see were dark, looming shapes closing in on her.

Eventually, night turned into day. The day when the town would find out how the new vice chancellor would fare in the spotlight of conducting the first Spinning House trial that was open to the public.

20

THE NEW
COURTROOM

It was the morning after the arrest of Daisy Hopkins. The clatter of
early morning industry was well under way. But something was different. An atmosphere of excitement was palpable. Already, the cold
breath of tradesmen hung in the air as they shared the electrifying news
that a young woman had been taken to the Spinning House the night
before. Speculation mounted as to how the new vice chancellor would
fare in the glare of a public trial inside the new Spinning House court.
Who, they wondered, would be prepared to come to the defence of the
inmate of the dreaded prison? A person brave enough to do that could
become a victim of the social and economic power of the university.

The noise on the busy streets in the centre of the town did not pene-
trate the tranquil surroundings of the Master's Lodge of Christ's College.
There, John Piele sat gazing out of the window as he worked his way
through a substantial breakfast. The clipped lawns of his private garden
were dusted with frost. It was going to be a chilly day.

His reverie was interrupted by the arrival of a note, penned that morning by Frederick Wallis, the proctor who'd arrested Daisy Hopkins.
It notified Piele that his presence was required at eleven o'clock to preside
over a trial at the Spinning House.

The news disrupted everything. For a fleeting moment, Piele didn't
know what to do or who to turn to. Still, he awaited the report, lingering
in the London offices of Wright & Scott, in answer to his questions about
procedural matters in the revised Spinning House courtroom. Hastily, he
penned a note to the university solicitor, Musgrave Francis, of Francis &
Francis. 'Come quickly!' was the tone of his plea. Despite being judge and
jury in his own court, the vice chancellor urgently needed legal advice.

Mrs Johnson, the assiduous matron of the Spinning House, who had lived on the premises for over thirty-seven years, was equally ruffled by the news that members of the public were to be admitted into her realm that morning. The heavy wooden doors of the prison were usually barred against the world, but that day, she worried that the whole world would want to want to enter her orderly domain. She didn't like it.

She'd had no instruction on who to let in and who to bar. Would she be in trouble for admitting journalists, or the accused family, she wondered? The event was bound to attract all sorts of dubious people.

University officials were struggling too. Despite notice having gone out at eight that morning that a solicitor was needed to defend the accused, it was proving difficult to find someone to fill that role. The solicitor who had at first agreed to take on the job had changed his mind. Speculation mounted that no solicitor would have the courage to fight for the rights of a victim of a Spinning House arrest.

Into this cauldron of uncertainty arrived a man of principle and certainty, a man who would achieve fame for his legal dexterity. Algernon Jasper Lyon, whose law practice was almost opposite the Spinning House, was appointed at the eleventh hour. The town could not have hoped for a better man.

Aged 36, Lyon had already made a name for himself. Cambridge born and bred, he'd attended the Perse School in the town and read Law at Queens' College, he was already the town's registrar and captain of the Fire Service. He'd been on the Board of Guardians at the workhouse and was a borough councillor. Despite being town and gown, in his election manifesto, the previous year, when standing as councillor for St Andrew the Less in Barnwell, he had vowed, 'If elected, I will do my best to promote the general welfare of the town at all times.' His rivals mocked him for being 'a friend of the working man'.

He used the short hour at his disposal to gather the Hopkins family. First, Mrs Hopkins got to work. She briefed Charles Hopkins on what had happened the previous evening and sent him to find the boy who had witnessed Daisy's arrest. A picture of the events leading up to the arrest were sketched out. There was no time to speak to the prisoner herself.

It was almost eleven o'clock when a flustered Mrs Johnson opened the Spinning House door to someone she knew for certain she could admit. In breezed the vice chancellor and a bevy of proctors – there to help him fathom his procedural rights in the new court. A short distance behind them came Algernon Lyon, accompanied by Charles Hopkins and Charles Camps.

'Sir, I've got reporters here,' said Mrs Johnson to one of the proctors. 'Should I let them in?' The two eager reporters who'd arrived early to bag a seat had been steered into a dark corridor, not the courtroom. Matron desperately need guidance about who to let in.

Lyon arrived in the new courtroom. It wasn't large and was bare of any ornamentation. A faint smell of paint clung in the damp air. He took a seat at the end of a table doubling as the court bench. He surveyed the room. He was shocked to see quite a crowd of onlookers at the far end of the room. They were penned in like wild animals behind 9ft iron bars. The design of the room suggested great thought had gone into the management of unruly members of the public – from inside and out. Its windows, which faced the street, were barred as if trouble were expected at any moment, and stale air was already collecting in the freshly whitewashed room.

But the town was holding its collective breath that morning, rather than its clenched fists. Lyon watched as the two reporters were escorted by a policeman to the pew-like seats in the main well of the court.

Vice Chancellor John Piele, splendid in his academic robes, took centre stage along the long table, proctors flanked their master's side. Lyon sat at one end, the university solicitor, Musgrave Francis, at the other. At the sight of Lyon, Francis hastily penned a note, sending it off with a messenger. Had the sight of Lyon, renowned for fighting for the underdog, unnerved Francis? Was he was calling in reinforcements?

Soon after eleven, the clerk of the court leaned towards the vice chancellor. He shared some information Lyon could not quite catch, resulting in John Piele clearing his throat, signalling his readiness to embark on the first open court at the Spinning Court, one where, for the first time on record, evidence was to be taken on oath and the prisoner represented by counsel.

It was a significant day – a magnificent day. One that Charles Henry Cooper, who, fifty years ago, had taken the first public stand against the evils of the Spinning House, would have been proud to have witnessed. A slight stutter caused a hesitation in Piele's speech, yet it only increased the gravity of his words when he spoke. 'B-bring the prisoner in,' he commanded.

Agnes, the under matron, ushered Daisy into the courtroom. It was Lyon's first sight of the girl he was there to defend. She was, he noticed, a delicate-looking girl. Her long, uncombed hair had been fastened back as best she could, troublesome strands pushed under the wide brim of her fawn-coloured hat. She was shown to a chair at the front of the room but told to stand. She seemed stunned. Almost robotic in her movements.

The reporters, sitting in the pew-like benches in the well of the courtroom, noted down every detail of what they later described as her 'fashionable attire' – a fetching navy-blue costume trimmed with gold edging. Unnoticed by them was the small tear in the seam of the gathers under the arm of her dress – a reminder, only to Daisy, of the aggressive treatment she had suffered the night before. She stood upright and alone among a throng of severe men in black gowns.

Surveying the prisoner though his thin, metal-framed glasses, Piele told her, 'You are charged with the offence of walking with a member of the university. How do you plead?'

All eyes shot in the direction of the prisoner. 'Not guilty, Sir,' came Daisy Hopkins' hesitant voice.

'I call the Reverend Frederic Wallis to ...' The vice chancellor was halted mid-sentence by Lyon.

'Under which authority do you take oaths?' Lyon wanted to know.

He was late to the proceedings that day, but he was prompt in spotting the first of many inconsistencies between a court run according to British law and one clinging to ancient privileges. Was the vice chancellor authorised to take oaths? Judges swore allegiance to Queen and Country to uphold English law; not something the vice chancellor had done.

'Why, my own.' The vice chancellor brushed off Lyon's challenge.

Wallis explained how he had come across a woman in the company of a member of the university the previous evening.

'Why is the man not named or present?' Lyon jumped in. 'He is a vital part of this trial. He is a key witness to the event. He should be here.'

'It is not necessary to name the man nor call him,' stated Wallis. Never had any man ever been required to give evidence. It was simply unheard of.

The vice chancellor agreed. 'The man is not on trial.'

'I would like it noted that you do not permit the man to be questioned,' Lyon insisted.

Suspecting trouble on this point, Francis penned another note, the outcome of which would soon be revealed.

'Was the prisoner acting in an immodest way when she was arrested?' Lyon asked Wallis.

'I didn't see the prisoner in the act of impropriety,' Wallis confessed, 'but I had received information from my constables that the prisoner had been guilty of an offence.' He paused, then added by way of explanation, 'My men knew her to be a prostitute.'

'I beg your pardon, can I speak?' protested Daisy. She was eager to defend her character.

'No,' the vice chancellor scolded. 'You are represented.'

A plea came from behind the bars of the public gallery. 'Gentlemen, she has a father who works hard to keep her!' It was Mr Hopkins, desperate to defend his daughter and the family's honour.

'Silence!' the vice chancellor, who wasn't used to being interrupted, barked.

Constable Kirby was sworn in. Lyon asked if he had seen anything improper take place.

'I saw nothing improper take place between the man and the girl, but I have seen her walking with men on former occasions,' Kirby was keen to divulge.

'And what was she doing at that time?' Lyon asked, an eyebrow slightly raised at the ridiculousness of such a statement. Kirby had to admit he hadn't ever witnessed her 'importuning men'.

Constable Mason was sworn. 'I've seen her walking with men, university men. I've seen her talking to them as if they were pals and nudging them at night.'

'And how did you know they were university men?' Lyon pressed.

'I knew because of their caps and gowns.'

'Other people might wear caps and gowns,' remarked Lyon, 'I have seen barristers in them. This is presumption on your part. What proof do you have that the accused was soliciting?'

'I would not go as far as to say I have actually heard the prisoner importuning men, but she has spoken to gentlemen as she passed by,' Mason confessed.

'And was she walking only with one man?' Lyon wanted to expose Kirby's and Mason's 'evidence' as being nothing more than speculation.

'I cannot say I saw her alone. Two or three would be walking together and she would have something to say to them,' a defensive Mason explained.

'Was she alone at these times?' asked Lyon.

'Sometimes she was in the company of other females.'

Lyon was satisfied. So far, he had failed to uncover any evidence of law breaking. But just before the hearing had begun that morning, Francis, the university solicitor, had recalled the existence of a document that could save the day. He'd summoned Mr Innes, Chief Superintendent of the Borough Police, to bring the register of known prostitutes in Cambridge. A week later, he would be berated by the town for succumbing to the bidding of the university when it was his duty to serve the town. But the poor man had been at a loss to know what to do. He confessed he knew of a university charter binding his office to submit to their will and didn't know what to do.

'There is a register of prostitutes in Cambridge …' Innes began.

'Is the prisoner's name on the list?' was all the vice chancellor wanted to know.

'It is,' Innes confirmed.

Lyon had heard of this book. 'And I wonder, could you tell me how that register is compiled?'

Innes explained that the register was kept for information. Statistics about prostitution were sent to the government annually.

'I cannot accept that register as proof,' Lyon declared. 'We have no evidence as to how those records are made. We must have direct evidence from individuals on that point.' His fight to run the court according to the law of the land earnt him applause from the crowd installed behind the iron bars, and later, in newsprint.

'It is compiled by an officer specially appointed to the task,' Innes defended the book. 'I've never known of any inaccuracies,' he said. 'Names are entered based on observation and personal enquiry.'

'And you know Daisy Hopkins?' Lyon enquired.

Innes admitted that although he knew the name Daisy Hopkins, he did not think he knew what she looked like.

'I believe there are many false returns upon such books,' Lyon argued. 'Names are entered on hearsay. This document does not constitute evidence.'

Yet the vice chancellor disagreed. 'The book can be accepted as evidence,' he announced, to the nodding approval of the proctors gathered around him.

'I bow to the decision of the court.' Lyon could do no other than concede, prompting a journalist from the *Cambridge Daily News* to remark that despite Mr Lyon querying almost every point, it 'was overruled with a cold cynicism that was simply sickening'.

Meanwhile, a messenger arrived in response to the university solicitor's second note. He shared the information with Musgrave Francis. What unorthodox procedure would he have to tackle next, Lyon wondered?

'It would appear, vice chancellor,' Francis announced, 'that we can produce the member of the university.'

The man seen with the prisoner in Tennis Court Road the night before had been persuaded to give evidence, something he would long regret. He must have assumed once he'd given his account of what had happened the previous night, he'd hear no more about it. He already faced a fine for not wearing his academicals on the night of Daisy's arrest. Perhaps he'd come to an arrangement with his college. Charles Russell was, at that point, a married undergraduate at Jesus College with a promising career in India ahead of him. He was an uncomfortable witness.

'I passed the prisoner in the street,' he told the court. 'She looked at me, and I spoke to her. I asked her if she could take me to her rooms.' The damning words came out in way that made them sound rehearsed.

'I don't think we need examine the witness further,' concluded the vice chancellor.

But Lyon didn't share the vice chancellor's confidence. He wanted clarification.

'You spoke to her first. Is that so?' he asked Russell.

'Yes,' replied Russell.

'Did she solicit you in any way?'

'No.'

This was the evidence the defence lawyer wanted to hear. It wasn't the accused who had been soliciting, it was the man. According to the law of the land, Daisy was innocent. As much as the vice chancellor believed in Daisy's guilt, Lyon had proved her innocence – according to the law of the land.

Before calling his witnesses, Lyon gave a summary of the situation. 'The charter that this case is taken on is not generally known. In fact, so far as I know, it is not printed nor is it available for purchase in any shop in Cambridge. Women committed under the charter must be "suspected of evil" and, so far, there is no evidence of that.' He declared that the prisoner might have been seen talking to townsmen and university men, but she had friends and relations living in the town, so it would be strange if she were not seen talking to them or walking with them. Regarding university men, his 'experience was that university men frequently spoke to girls'. The remark was met with loud applause. 'Not only did they speak to them,' he was at pains to point out, 'but they frequently insisted on walking with them, often against their will. There is no evidence that this girl was "suspected of evil" and I will prove this,' he concluded.

He called 17-year-old Charles Camps.

'I saw the prisoner last night. She was alone when I first saw her,' Camps said.

'What happened next?' asked Lyon.

'I saw the Bulldogs with her. They pressed her against some railings in Lensfield Road. Then, they took her past the Catholic cathedral. She shouted at me to fetch her father and mother.'

'What sort of character does the prisoner have?' Lyon asked.

'She bears a very good character. I do not know that she is a prostitute. From what I know of her, she is a well-conducted, orderly woman.'

Daisy's brother Charles was called. He worked at the Criterion Billiard Rooms as a billiard ball maker (he would be sacked later that day due to his association with the prisoner, despite his employer giving him a good character). Daisy's eyes fixed on her brother as he stood before the vice chancellor, wearing what she knew to be his best clothes.

'I never heard of her being a prostitute,' he said in an uneasy voice. 'She has a father and mother at home who maintain her. I've never heard about her doing anything immoral. It is not true she walks the streets for the purpose of soliciting …'

'As far as you know,' interrupted the vice chancellor.

'She used to attend St Matthew's Sunday school,' Charles told Lyon. 'She was under the notice of Reverent Ford about six months ago and bore a good reputation.'

Lyon asked if the court could adjourn so he could subpoena Reverend Ford, who might hold vital character evidence about the accused.

'No, no, no!' the vice chancellor replied.

Lyon asked if he could call the accused to give her account; she would contest the evidence that she had agreed to take Russell to her rooms.

'It is utterly inconceivable that Russell would have come there with any other intention than to speak the truth. No one could contradict his evidence.' The vice chancellor ridiculed the very question.

'It will be contradicted by the prisoner herself,' Lyon repeated.

'The prisoner can take the witness stand. But only to make a statement,' relented the vice chancellor. Already, in the eyes of the university, they had yielded enough to the law of the land. This court had adequately dealt with thousands of women over the decades. What more did the town want? Witnesses had been sworn and heard; the accused had legal representation. The girl, of dubious reputation, had been out at night. It was blatantly clear that she was guilty, believed one section of those present that morning.

'Why can't the accused have the same freedom as others to give evidence?' Lyon wanted to know.

The young woman, it appeared to many, had to be convicted at all costs.

Daisy readied to speak. She was thinking fast. She must prove her innocence. She couldn't survive another night in the cold and damp of the Spinning House. She had to give a convincing version of the events of the previous evening. She refused to be forever tarnished by the events of the previous night. She stood tall and spoke clearly as she gave her version of what had happened the night before.

'There were three women in Tennis Court Road on the night of my arrest,' she explained. 'One wearing a hat very similar to mine. It is all a case of mistaken identity. I had only been showing the man the way.'

Barred from questioning his client's version of events, no other version of what happened that night was ever heard. Lyon could do no more. Daisy returned to her seat. All eyes travelled to the face of the vice chancellor, who took a moment to confer with his proctors. Nods signalled accord.

'The charges against you are proved,' he announced. 'I sentence you to fourteen days.'

Stunned, Daisy cried out, 'It wasn't me at all. I was only showing him the way!' A wild hysteria took hold of her as Agnes stepped forward to return her to the cells. 'Keep your hands off me! I insist upon seeing my father. What am I going to jail for? I am innocent!'

'Come along ...' Agnes kindly coaxed as she placed a guiding hand on Daisy's back.

'Let me alone!' Daisy screamed, trying to shake herself free. 'Get out of my road or I will knock you out! What have I done to deserve this? I knew nothing about it until that beastly man Kirby came up last night and punched and knocked me about!'

Daisy's father and brother rushed from behind the iron bars separating the public from the well of the court. 'My daughter is under medical treatment with a quinsy,' Mr Hopkins pleaded with the vice chancellor.

'She is under the doctor's hands, Sir,' Charles Hopkins repeated his father's plea. 'I can get you a certificate.'

'The case is over,' announced the vice chancellor as he swept out of a room stuffy with stale air and undignified hysterics.

'I'm not in a fit state to lay in those damp cells,' he heard Daisy cry out as he reached the corridor outside the courtroom. 'I lay there shivering all night, I won't go. I won't go!' she yelled. 'I insist upon a doctor being sent for. If I am put in those nasty damp cells, I will kill myself!'

The horror of the sudden knowledge that she was about to spend two weeks locked up alone in the damp conditions of the Spinning House cannot be underestimated. Daisy was a young woman used to living alongside the crowded clatter of working-class life in Barnwell. But there was no escape. Still raging, she was removed from the courtroom. Agnes led her, followed by her father and brother, to a small room. Lyon followed. He wanted to help in any way he could. Now the truth of how the vice chancellor's court worked had been exposed, Lyon was even more determined to see an end to it.

As Daisy was comforted by her father and brother in a small room close to the courtroom, Lyon asked for a doctor to be called to establish if Daisy was strong enough to withstand the conditions inside the prison. Hopefully, a doctor would confirm it wasn't a fit place to lock up women. This fragile-looking girl already looked hollow-eyed and weak.

Meanwhile, the vice chancellor, accompanied by Musgrave Francis and the matron, gathered in another part of the prison to complete the Committal document. It must have been a rushed process because two highly educated men failed to notice a serious error in what they signed and sealed:

To the Keeper of the Spinning House, or House of Correction, in the University and Town of Cambridge.

Whereas Daisy Hopkins hath been apprehended by the Rev. Frederic Wallis, one of the Proctors of said University, within the limit and jurisdiction thereof, and hath this day been brought before me and charged with walking with a member of the University in a certain public street of the town and suburbs of Cambridge, and within the precincts of the said University, which charge, as well upon the information of the said Proctor, as upon the examination of the said Frederic Wallis, and after having heard what the said Frederic Wallis had to allege in her defence, I do adjudge to be true: These are therefore to require and command you to receive into your custody the said Daisy Hopkins, and her safely to keep in your said Spinning House for 14 days. Given under my hand and seal at Cambridge this third day of December 1891.

John Piele, Master of Christ's College and Vice Chancellor of the University of Cambridge.
Agnes Johnson, Keeper of the Spinning House.

The fact that the name Fredric Wallis had been inserted in the place of Daisy Hopkins was an error of no consequence, but that she was charged with 'walking with a member of the University in a certain public street of the town' would prove disastrous for the new vice chancellor.

As Mr Hopkins and Charles were forced to say goodbye to the prisoner, Charles took Lyon aside. 'Sir, please do whatever you can to free my sister. I will find the money somehow,' he promised, as he pressed half a crown into the solicitor's hand.

But as news broke of how the vice chancellor ran his court, Charles Hopkins wasn't the only person wanting his sister's freedom. The document, still warm from its wax seal, would soon be used in evidence against the man whose right hand still carried a small smudge of the ink that had wrongly condemned the prisoner.

21

THE PRISONER

Ashiver ran through Daisy Hopkins as she gazed at what had been placed on the bed in her prison cell. Tears streamed down her pale face as her fingers fumbled to undo the small buttons fastening her fashionable blue bodice and matching skirt. Before her lay the regulation prison dress.

'I'll be back soon.' Agnes tossed the words over her shoulder as she hurried to attend to the stove in the prison corridor. 'Make a neat pile of your own clothes,' she ordered the new prisoner.

Daisy was in no rush to feel the folds of the uniform fall against her delicate skin, but the chill of the room obliged her to hasten to fasten the ties.

'Read me the rules,' Agnes commanded on returning for her fireside duties. Two printed cards hung side by side on one of the cell walls. They had not been placed there for decorative effect. 'I told Matron I'd hear you say them,' Agnes urged a hesitant Daisy on.

'The prisoner is to bathe and put on the dress prepared for her,' Daisy began. 'The prisoner will occupy a separate cell and follow such employment or means of instruction as the prison officers will command. The prisoner will keep her cell clean. The cells will be locked from eight at night till eight the next morning in winter – seven in summer.' She stopped to confirm with Agnes that she would be allowed a night commode, before continuing, 'Meals are laid down in the Dietary. Food and drink are not to be brought in.' Her voice fell to a choked whisper. 'The prisoner will not see friends or family except by written order of the vice chancellor, or his deputed officer, and only then for a quarter of an hour in the presence of the matron.' Daisy paused to give the tears welling up in her eyes time to roll down her cheeks, before reading the final rule. 'Punishment for bad behaviour or neglect of these rules is solitary confinement with bread and water for a period of not more than three days.'

The second card hanging on the cell was the Dietary. It listed the meagre rations a prisoner could expect. Agnes instructed Daisy to read it, but not out loud. Breakfast consisted of 6oz bread with a weekly allowance of 2oz tea, 7oz sugar and 1½ pints of milk. Dinner varied according to the number of inmates, but for four days of the week 5oz meat was provided, with bread and potatoes, the other days, soup, bread and a 12oz suet pudding was cooked. Supper consisted of 6oz of bread or 1 pint of oatmeal gruel. The list did not arouse Daisy's delicate appetite.

Mr Algernon Lyon might have lost the fight that morning, but he had the appetite to win the battle. Back in his office, he instigated a forensic search of the detailed wording of the charter. It paid off. He spotted a chink in the vice chancellor's armour. Daisy Hopkins was, it turned out, a victim of a miscarriage of justice, and Lyon could prove it.

Meanwhile, at one o'clock in the afternoon, Daisy sat in her prison dress quelling a swelling revulsion in her stomach. Agnes had just placed the regulation dinner before her. Any appetite she might have had was lost as she poked the fatty meat – she thought it was 'lights' – the slang for offal – with three unpeeled, boiled potatoes. Daisy wanted a cup of sweet tea, but none was offered.

At three o'clock, Mr James Hough, the prison doctor, arrived. Daisy sat warming herself by the stove near her cell. A pale mess of tear-stained face looked up at him.

'You are unwell?' It was a statement not a question.

The sight of the doctor triggered fresh tears. She buried her face in her already sodden handkerchief. 'Yes,' she croaked. 'I have the quinsy.'

The doctor examined her. First, he took her pulse, then her temperature. She was a delicate-looking girl, he observed. 'Can I see your throat?' he asked.

There, he detected an inflammation of not just her tonsils but nearby organs. In his professional view, the symptoms of the quinsy were past their peak but still of concern. 'Your throat is unwell,' he confirmed. 'I will send for some medicine.'

'Mr Rygate has been attending me, Sir,' she explained. 'His medicine isn't here.'

Mr Hough sent Agnes to fetch a gargle from the chemist. He added to the list a bitter tonic containing quassia and gentian to help settle her stomach and her nerves. He also prescribed a daily turn around the prison yard. 'I'll visit tomorrow,' he said.

While Daisy started to come to terms with the horror of her situation, two men were scrutinising the wording of the ancient charter. Lyon had recruited the help of Dr John Cooper, a town councillor, magistrate, celebrated barrister and close friend. Who else would anyone turn to?

John Cooper was the son of Charles Henry Cooper, the man who had conducted the inquest into the untimely death of Elizabeth Howe in 1846. He was the younger brother of Thompson Cooper, who had helped in the fight to compensate Emma Kemp for false imprisonment in 1860, when the omnibus she was travelling in was halted by proctors and policemen and she and her fellow female passengers were forced inside the Spinning House.

Cooper was a law graduate from Trinity Hall. He'd been called to the Bar in 1868, but lived in Cambridge, playing a prominent part in municipal affairs and revising his father's *Annals of Cambridge* – to which he added a fifth volume. He was referred to as an 'aggressive Liberal', who wanted to see an end to class government, or 'grandmotherly government', as he called it. As a lenient magistrate, he claimed that nine-tenths of the petty crime he was called to judge was the result of drunkenness. It's not surprising to find that he was a great supporter of the Temperance Movement. It would have been impossible to find two more dogged men determined to bring about the downfall of the Spinning House.

The next day, newspapers from all corners of the land broke the story of the latest Spinning House scandal in Cambridge. Coming so soon after the antics of Jane Elsden, the latest tale triggered a blistering attack on the university. How, people demanded to know, in an enlightened England, was it possible for the vice chancellor of a university to sentence a 17-year-old girl to fourteen days' imprisonment for the crime of speaking to an undergraduate?

At ten o'clock on that Friday morning, as news of the arrest was being debated in all corners of the kingdom, the prison chaplain arrived to see Daisy. The two talked for over an hour. What they said is not recorded, but it stirred Daisy to make a request.

'I want some work,' she told Agnes.

Agnes was uncertain what work she might offer the prisoner.

'I don't care what I do,' pressed Daisy.

Agnes wondered if the chaplain had spoken of repentance. She might have been right.

'I'd like to scrub out the courtroom.'

It was an odd request, thought Agnes, but she agreed.

It took Daisy half an hour to scrub out the courtroom. Yet, the thirty minutes Daisy spent on her knees gave her a chance to reflect on the events of the previous day. She realised she was innocent in the eyes of the law; Lyon was right about that. But could he secure her release? She remembered her brother's words as he left her earlier that day, 'I'll do all I can to free you.' But what had she been doing that night?

She must stick to her story. It was all a case of mistaken identity. She was showing the man the way. She had been to Newnham to see her fiancé; he wasn't there. She would get out of that damp and cold place somehow.

The question of Daisy Hopkins' liberty was being debated by many that same morning as they devoured the headlines of their daily papers. The *Cambridge Evening News* summoned up the sentiments of much of the nation:

Once more the Cambridge university authorities have outraged public decency by an intolerable sentence upon a young girl accused of being in the company of an undergraduate. We hoped we'd seen the last of the academical tyranny practiced upon the townsfolk of Cambridge. Until this survivor of the dark ages is abolished it will be our task to impress upon the government the supreme necessity of depriving the university authorities of their ill needed privileges of oppressing innocent women.

The London newspaper *The Star* called the Spinning House 'the black hole of Cambridge'.

A Cambridge correspondent called Binky Baldwin asked readers of the *Cambridge Independent*, 'Do the people of Cambridge possess any backbone or not? Mr Charles Russell of Jesus College had said "She looked at me and I spoke to her. I asked her if she could take me to her rooms".' Was there, Binky Baldwin wanted to know, a law, 'by Charter or Common Law', that prosecuted men who solicited girls of 17 or 18? He demanded a law to prosecute such men. 'The person who debauches is worse than the girl,' he claimed. 'I am a poor man,' he admitted, but promised to donate £1 towards the cost of such prosecution.

He wasn't alone in offering financial support for an action against the university. The Personal Rights Association at 3 Victoria Street, Westminster, contacted Mr Lyon to offer funds to proceed with a legal case to 'test or call public attention to the jurisdiction of the vice chancellor'.

The Social wing of the Salvation Army jumped into action too. A letter arrived on the desk of the Home Secretary from Colonel James Baker, of the Criminal Investigation Department of the Salvation Army, whose officers had been instrumental in the release of Jane Elsden. He promised to petition for the release of 'Miss Hopkins'. He wrote, 'Our experienced officer at Cambridge is making a full investigation and has already interviewed the poor girl's mother and friends.' He promised to 'lay the full facts' before the Home Secretary and offered to take the girl into one of Mrs Bramwell-Booth's homes so that 'she may be saved and not branded a prostitute due to the stigma of prison.'

On Saturday, 5 December, Lyon arrived at the Spinning House with good news. 'I believe I can free you,' he told Daisy, as the pair sat in the small, whitewashed room she had been taken to on the night of her arrival.

'I won't go away!' cried out Daisy, remembering that Jane Elsden was sent to London.

'No, no,' reassured Lyon. He didn't go into the full detail of his plans but explained that she had been charged with 'walking with a member of the university'. The original charter stipulated only women found walking with a member of the university for the purpose of 'evil' – a coy word for prostitution – could be imprisoned. The committal paperwork only stated that Daisy had been 'walking with a member of the university', a slip-up that Lyon and Cooper were determined to exploit. They planned to petition for a writ of habeas corpus for unlawful imprisonment.

Lyon explained to Daisy that, under English law, people deprived of their liberty due to arrest and detention were entitled to challenge the lawfulness of their detention. He believed he could prove her imprisonment was unlawful.

Everyone had known that the first public hearing of a Spinning House trial was going to cause a hullabaloo, whoever was arrested. What no one could have anticipated was how far Lyon and Cooper would go in their determination to rid the town of the Spinning House.

On the same Saturday that Lyon spoke to Daisy inside the Spinning House, an officer from the Salvation Army arrived at the front door of 36 Gold Street to speak to Mrs Hopkins. The officer had been asked to make a report on the living conditions of the Hopkins family. She noted that the house in Gold Street was 'an ordinary working man's home'. The officer had awkward questions to ask.

'Does Daisy go out at night?' she asked.

'Oh no,' said Mrs Hopkins.

'Does she have any work?' queried the officer.

'She's a delicate girl,' Mrs Hopkins explained. 'We keep her at home. She's been under the doctor's hands for some time. He'd have granted a certificate to confirm her ill health if he'd been allowed.' Mrs Hopkins was quite indignant about the way her daughter had been treated by the vice chancellor. A doctor's note would have proved she was suffering from the quinsy.

'And the rest of your family, Mrs Hopkins. Where are they?'

It was established that there were six sons and three daughters in the family. Daisy's father had been a shepherd for nearly fifty years at Sutton, Cambridge. They had moved to Ely, then Cambridge, after the father's work dried up. Mrs Hopkins was proud to tell the officer that her son Arthur lived and worked for the Reverend Spencer of Leamington, Warwickshire. 'He's been with them above thirty years.' Mrs Hopkins was keen to make much of the clerical connection.

Son Alfred was a captain of the militia. He lived at Lymington, Hampshire. Each of the other brothers worked away from home. They were all doing well, according to Mrs Hopkins, who forgot to mention Charles Hopkins' recent sacking due to his sister's recent infamy. She added that Alice was married and Lydia had gone to live in London.

In her report to Colonel Baker, the officer concluded that the family was a respectable one. But after questioning the Hopkinses' neighbours, added she'd heard that Daisy Hopkins was believed to be prostitute, albeit one of the more genteel in character. In the family's favour, she stated that none of the daughters had been summoned to the Spinning House before and she highlighted the fact that a brother worked for a clergyman. She stressed that the family were greatly concerned about Daisy, who was a frail young woman who'd been under the doctor for several years. The family were worried about the damp cells the vice chancellor had sent Daisy to.

While Mrs Hopkins tried to convince people of the family's respectability, two barristers were being engaged by Lyon to contest the legality of Daisy's detention. First was Dr John Cooper, whose forensic knowledge of the Elizabethan charter under which Daisy had been detained could not be rivalled. It is quite possible he waivered his legal fee to enable the hiring of the second barrister – a man who came highly recommended.

That man was Mr Harry Bodkin Poland, a noted barrister who'd gained fame in the notorious Chocolate Cream Poisoning case. It was his skill that commuted a death sentence to one of life imprisonment for Christiana Edmunds, who'd purchased confectionery from a shop in Brighton, laced it with strychnine and returned it for sale, killing a young boy, as well causing illness in many others. Later, it was agreed that Christiana, whose family had a history of mental illness, should be moved to a lunatic asylum.

On the morning of Tuesday, 8 December, Mr Algernon Jasper Lyon confidently stepped onto a train that would transport him to London. It was the day the case for habeas corpus was being placed before the Lord Chief Justice in the Royal Courts of Justice.

That morning, with few people present, the Lord Chief Justice, having heard the arguments from both sides, announced a full hearing the following Friday. It would be a day that would make legal history.

22

HABEAS CORPUS

The gales that had been devastating the country for days had dwindled to gusts just strong enough to make the queue of horse-drawn cabs skittish outside the Royal Courts of Justice in the Strand. Just over nine years before, on 4 December 1882, Queen Victoria had declared open this gothic temple devoted to the law, but already London's heavy, swirling soot veiled the shining splendour of its original Portland stone. However, few were looking up. Hats were in danger of leaving heads as visitors hastened through the regal arches of the main entrance into the Great Hall. It was Friday, 11 December 1891, and seats in the public gallery were in great demand.

Mr Lyon was among those entering the Great Hall that day, and he had only one thing on his mind. Would his legal team – paid for by public subscription – secure justice for Daisy Hopkins?

Those snapping up seats in the public gallery of the Lord Chancellor's Court were looking forward to witnessing the unusual prospect of some of the greatest legal minds in the country fighting over the prospects of a young, working-class girl. Among them sat Vice Chancellor Dr John Piele, with his clerk, Mr Musgrave Francis, and the proctor, Reverend Frederic Wallis, who had arrested Daisy just over a week ago.

Daisy wasn't there to witness the occasion: the case centred on the wording on the charge sheet, not the prisoner herself. 'The Spinning House Victim', as many newspapers had branded Daisy, was settling into her ninth day of captivity, yearning for it to be her last. Could Lyon really persuade those important men in London to free her? She hoped he could.

The Lord Chief Justice, Lord Coleridge, took his seat at 10.30 a.m. The case had caused great interest outside the realms of academia, proving it to be a more than equal attraction to another notorious one that was taking place in an adjacent courtroom. There, another crowd had gathered to witness the high drama of a divorce case between a famous theatrical couple, Miss Margaret Florence St John and her flamboyant but adulterous French actor husband, Claude Marius Duplany. The line of defence was to implicate unfaithfulness on the part of Miss St John.

Back in the Lord Chancellor's Court, it was clear that the Vice Chancellor of Cambridge University wasn't planning to face defeat. The financial resources of the university had been quarried to find for him a great deal of talent – and with it, a great deal of confidence. The Attorney General, Sir Richard Webster, an alumnus of Trinity College Cambridge, was appointed to defend Dr Piele, aided by Mr Arthur Cohen QC, an alumnus of Magdalene College Cambridge.

Lyon heard the nearby Church of St Clements Danes strike the half hour as he settled into his seat. It was hard to gauge which way judgment would fall. The university had packed a punch by selecting the Attorney General to defend them, but modern men, outside the rarefied world of ancient tradition, knew change was on the horizon, change that the government could force on an institution that needed to prove its relevance in a modern world.

First, that morning, Mr Poland, briefed by Lyon, rose to address His Lordship. 'This girl has done nothing wrong. That is, to the mind of anyone not an official of the university,' he explained. 'And,' he quipped, 'is very upset at finding herself in prison.' Poland had an elegantly long nose that he always seemed to be gazing down when he spoke. The physical gesture suited the contempt he conjured when addressing his legal opponents:

Dr Piele, the Vice Chancellor of Cambridge University, is a man of the highest personal character. But he has made a series of unfortunate blunders. He convicted a girl of walking with an undergraduate, a law unknown to man. A book listing alleged prostitutes was brought in by the police which, as every lawyer knows, is no evidence. The man who she was accused of accosting swore that it was he who accosted her. Dr Piele would not allow the girl to make a statement on oath or be examined in court by her solicitor, he would not grant a subpoena for a witness as to the good character of the girl and declined to adjourn the hearing so evidence of her good character could be obtained.

He made the legal insufficiency of the vice chancellor's court crystal clear, declaring:

It debased the law to send to prison a respectable young woman. The whole of this academical tyranny over persons not belonging to the university is an utter abuse and ought to be swept away. Let the Dons punish their own if they can't restrain them.

Cooper spoke next, setting out the simple facts of the case. It was a satisfying moment. Here he was, in a prestigious London courtroom, among the best legal minds in the country, fighting the battle his father had started. Victory was tantalisingly close. He began:

Before any court in the land can charge someone with an offence, it has to be clear what that offence is, and, if they have the authority to charge them with it. The charge, as it appears on the chart sheet for Daisy Hopkins, is no charge within the four corners of the university charter.

The Attorney General spoke next. 'I appear on behalf of the Vice Chancellor of Cambridge University,' he confirmed. 'The matter here has been most distinctly misunderstood,' he explained with the air of someone already slightly bored by the proceedings; so sure he was to triumph. In wood-panelled chambers close to where he now stood, he and his legal friend, Arthur Cohen QC, had been in deep conversation for several days about how to argue their way out of the hole the vice chancellor had unwittingly stumbled into. The Attorney General was ready to refute any wrongdoing on the part of his client:

The suggestion is that the vice chancellor convicted this young woman of an offence described as 'walking with a member of the university'. Over the years proctors have used these same words to mean that a girl has been out for immoral purposes. The charge was, in fact, that she was found in the company of an undergraduate for immoral purposes, although, I agree that was not what was written down.

He advocated that it was, in fact, everyone else's fault for not understanding something so plain and simple. 'It was true,' he said, 'that over the years vice chancellors have often used the wording "arrested for walking with an undergraduate". But everyone knew what was really meant.'

But the wording was not legally binding under any law, even the loathed charter. There was no misunderstanding in the minds of Lyon, Cooper and Poland about the vice chancellor's slip-up.

When the court broke for luncheon, there was much speculation under the high gothic ceilings about how the case would end.

Returning for the afternoon session, the Lord Chief Justice said he'd read the account of the trial as portrayed in the *Cambridge Independent* newspaper. He had read affidavits from the vice chancellor and Wallis. He had also read a translation of the charter and the case of *Kemp vs Neville*, but there were questions to be answered. 'Must not the vice chancellor, as was done in *Kemp vs Neville* show an offence within the terms of the charter?' He referred to the case of Emma Kemp who, it was acknowledged, had been wrongly arrested, yet according to the terms of the charter, had behaved 'suspiciously' and so was guilty.

'No doubt,' replied the Attorney General. 'But I can show such an offence would have been written in later.'

'But surely the charge must be made before evidence is taken on it?' queried Lord Coleridge. 'It seems that this girl was tried on a charge different from the one she was accused of.'

This was the core issue. The legal paperwork stated that Daisy had been arrested for 'walking with an undergraduate', yet she had been on trial for 'walking with an undergraduate for immoral purposes'.

'I find that the wording used was not legally sufficient,' he announced. 'The prisoner must be discharged, and the wording used in this case must never be used again. It must say that the person is "suspected of evil".'

This was a win for Lyon, Cooper and almost every inhabitant of Cambridge, as well as for the young woman waiting in the gloom of Cell 10. A few hours later, Daisy Hopkins was a free woman.

The case of habeas corpus for Daisy Hopkins made legal history. Even today, law students learn the vital fact that a suspect must be charged with, and tried for, the same crime. In 1999 it was the topic of Lord Justice Simon Brown's 'Annual Lecture to the Law Bar Association'. The importance of the correct wording in any charge document must be robust enough to stand scrutiny.

Back in Cambridge, at six o'clock on the evening of 11 December 1891, Mrs Hopkins arrived at the Spinning House to take her daughter home.

As the vice chancellor sought legal advice about shoring up his paperwork for future Spinning House trials, undergraduates at Cambridge changed the words of a popular song. The new version was chanted with glee at many sporting gatherings. The final match between town and gown was about to kick off:

Do ye ken John Piele and his learned court,
Do ye ken John Piele wi' his shrift so short,
Do ye ken John Piele when he's making sport
For the dons and Masters of Cambridge?
Yes, I ken John Piele and Butler too,
And the Proctors who prowl wi' their sleuthhounds true.
But I'm thinking they'll find there is payment due
For the sport they've been making at Cambridge
Then ye ken John Piele, and ye ken his games
Wi' the charter that dates from our guid King James,
And mayhap ye ken the unproven names
He stamped on his victim at Cambridge
And ye'll also ken how he tried the case:
Oh, the Spinning House is a fine braw place,
And it's there they'll teach you the means of grace,
Will the dons and the Masters of Cambridge!

H.M.

23

THE REVENGE

The fourteen days between the release of Daisy Hopkins and Christmas Eve 1891 were frantic. Lyon's and Cooper's rousing victory at the Royal Courts of Justice galvanised them to stop at nothing to rid the town of the prowling proctors and the Spinning House prison.

Meanwhile, the gossips in Gold Street, going about their Christmas errands, noticed newspaper reporters, Mr Lyon, and later, his clerk knocking on Daisy Hopkins' door. Rumour had it they were inside for quite some time. What were they planning?

Speculation was rife. The affronted words of Mrs Hopkins appeared in the *Cambridge Independent*, testifying to the harsh treatment of her delicate daughter inside the Spinning House. 'She was half starved,' she said. 'When she came out, she was in a worse condition than when she went in.'

But the question being debated behind the doors of the Hopkinses' home was if Daisy could be coaxed into pressing charges against the Reverend Wallis for wrongful arrest. Compensation was mentioned.

Could the pursuit of compensation change the family's fortunes? Daisy wasn't sure, but gossip about her was contagious. On venturing beyond her door, someone always had something to say to her. Remarks about her reputation landed in front and behind her as she went about her errands. She'd got above herself, with her fine clothes. Many were jealous of her new-found infamy. Cruel words cut. Her dreams of finding a nice boy, one who wouldn't knock her about, vanished the day her arrest became public. Soon she realised she did, in fact, have a great deal to be compensated for; then she wanted revenge.

On the evening of 18 December, in the council chamber of the Town Hall, Dr John Cooper prepared to address a packed meeting of borough councillors. He knew from the history books that negotiations with the university over the terms of the charter would be stalled and diluted until they fizzled out, as had been the case for calls for reform following the cases of Elizabeth Howe, Emma Kemp and Jane Elsden. 'I believe it is the wishes of the ratepayers of Cambridge that we fight for a Parliamentary Bill to put an end to university jurisdiction,' he proclaimed, to the sound of rousing cheers.

Since his late father had stood in the same building over thirty years ago, fighting for the end of the continued interference of the proctors in the lives of people who were not members of the university, the population of Cambridge had risen to beyond 10,000. So, too, had the number of those who were permitted to vote. Within days, in every corner of the town, notices signed by prominent men in the town were pasted to lampposts and tied to railings. They read:

To the Worshipful Mayor of the Borough of Cambridge.

We the undersigned Ratepayers of Cambridge do respectfully ask you to call a public meeting at an early date to consider the exceptional powers possessed by the university in regard of the Spinning House and to pass a resolution thereupon, and we further respectfully ask you to preside.

Straight away, the mayor announced a meeting would take place at eight o'clock on the evening of Wednesday, 30 December.

As Cooper galvanised the borough council into action, he and Lyon met to discuss a legal action for wrongful arrest against Wallis, the proctor who had ordered Daisy Hopkins into the Spinning House. What annoyed the two men most was they knew undergraduates routinely haunted the streets of Barnwell after dark. No steps were taken to seize those men. Yet when a woman walked in the streets close to the colleges at night, she risked arrest every step of the way.

By the afternoon of Christmas Eve, Lyon, aided by Cooper, was ready to strike a second blow against the tyranny of the university. Before he closed the door of Messrs Lyon & Cade, solicitors, of 21 St Andrew's Street, in readiness to head home for the festive season, he had sent a clerk to deliver a sealed letter to Reverend Wallis. It was a letter that, despite the season, did not bring glad tidings of joy.

That afternoon, as Wallis slid his letter knife through the envelope of the official-looking letter he later referred to as 'a queer kind of Christmas card', he was stunned. The document instructed him that Miss Daisy Hopkins was seeking damages for false imprisonment. In the letter, Lyon advocated that an offer of £130 – the cost of the high court proceedings – might quietly settle the matter. If not, full legal proceedings would follow. A troubled Wallis retreated to his study.

On Christmas Day, he penned a note to the vice chancellor. What was he to do?

Dr Piele was wondering the same, but for a different reason. Abusive letters addressed to the vice chancellor had been arriving at Christ's College. One came from 'Tit for Tat', accusing Piele of being 'an infamous blackguard'.

The two men had underestimated the rage spreading across the country about the university's determination to cling to their 'privilege' to arrest and imprison women on the flimsiest of evidence and their total disregard of the law of the land. The tide of public opinion was going against them. But inside their cloistered world, they were yet to comprehend that a new century of thinking was just around the corner.

As these events unfolded, Cooper and Lyon, along with most of the inhabitants of the town, watched the thermometer fall, first to freezing point then well below. The festive period coincided with the ice-skating season, reports of frost – perfect conditions for ice skating – and time to take a break from their battle. The cold conditions provided a temporary thaw in town and gown relations as both camps assembled on the banks of the River Cam.

On 28 December, Lyon prepared to steward the annual National Skating Association half-mile race held on Linga Fen, near Grantchester. Competitive skating was in his blood. His father had been a renowned amateur skater.

On that cold Monday morning, skaters from all over the country took part in heats to win the grand title of champion skater. Mr William Loveday of Winey, near Ely, took the title, beating Mr S.S. Burlington, a Yorkshireman from Settle. For a few short and cold days, senior members of the gown – the young scholars at risk of corruption had returned home for Christmas – were in excited harmony as they watched the competitors race along the frozen flooded Fen.

When Lyon and Cooper grabbed a moment to speak during the hectic clamour of the great annual sporting event, Cooper asked Lyon if he'd had a reply from Wallis. He hadn't, but both hoped Wallis would settle the matter out of court. They agreed that, whoever or whatever Daisy might be, she had committed no crime according to the law of the land on the night of her arrest.

As Piele and Wallis walked the mile or so from their colleges towards Grantchester, they too mulled over the matter of Daisy Hopkins. 'Your jurisdiction is unaffected by the ruling,' Wallis remarked, as they talked about the recent High Court judgment against them.

'I won't flinch from a fight if I have to,' Piele said of the proposed action against Wallis. 'I will see you get the best defence,' he promised.

Three days later, on New Year's Eve, the Hopkins family gathered round the hearth of 36 Gold Street. What a month it had been. Charles Hopkins was eager to read snippets from a report in the *Cambridge Chronicle* about the meeting that had been held inside the large chamber of the Guildhall the previous night:

> There were turbulent proceedings in the large reception room of the Town Hall. Dr Cooper gave a history of Town and Gown relations. Objections to the arrest and incarceration of women inside the Spinning House had gone before, he said. It was due to a Charter from the time of Queen Elizabeth, later confirmed by Act of Parliament.

'That old Charter got me inside the Spinning House!' Daisy said.

'Listen to this,' Charles cried out. 'Dr Cooper said, "As a university man I feel ashamed when I hear of such doings against the liberty of women living in Cambridge."'

'So, he should,' Mrs Hopkins, who was lapping up every moment of the rumpus her daughter was causing, chipped in.

'Someone asked if it was true that the Chief Constable, Mr Innes, had to keep a book of suspected prostitutes to send to government?' (Criticism of Mr Innes' appearance with the book that condemned Daisy Hopkins would long haunt him.) 'Guess what the mayor said?' asked Charles, '"I've spoken to a Member of Parliament on that matter and can report that no such evidence has been required since 1869."'

'And listen to this,' said Charles, as he reached the end of several columns of dense newspaper print. '"Someone at the meeting shouted out that the vice chancellor had the power to deprive people of their liberty, but not the necessary legal training to preside over a court."'

'Hear, hear!' cried the family.

'And our Daisy will finish them off,' declared Mrs Hopkins.

The town, together with the rest of the country, had spent most of 1891 consumed by the cases of Jane Elsden and Daisy Hopkins. Demands for the revision of the ancient rights and privileges of the university were certainly in the air. The new year, only hours away, looked tantalisingly promising.

24

BOGUS DAISY AND THE CAUSE CÉLÈBRE

During the first week of January 1892, the fight for justice for Daisy Hopkins moved up a notch. National newspapers revealed the news that the 'girl recently concerned in the Spinning House case' was poised to serve a writ against Reverend Mr Frederic Wallis. She was about to claim £1,000 for false imprisonment.

Her solicitor stated that, among other things, the prison was filthy and cold. His client had been forced to scrub out the courtroom, until the prison doctor put an end to such inhumane proceedings. And servants at a house in the vicinity had thrown objectionable remarks at her while she walked in the prison yard.

Daisy's account of her time in the Spinning House, the one presented to her solicitor, differed from the one remembered by Agnes, the under matron. But truth became irrelevant to those caught up in *Hopkins vs Wallis* as they began to wage their bitter battle.

As gossip mounted about the forthcoming trial, *The Times* newspaper speculated that the university would use its power and influence to shift the trial away from Cambridge, where a sympathetic jury was likely to sway the outcome and rioters might bloody the streets. 'The trial will take place in Norwich,' they first reported, then London was suggested. In the event, neither had the pleasure of hosting the celebrated event.

On Wednesday, 17 February, further fuel was added to the fire. A young woman charged with being drunk and disorderly and assaulting a police constable in Gracechurch Street, London, said she was Jane Elsden, but on being brought before the lord mayor at the Mansion House, recalled her name was Daisy Hopkins, a milliner from Gold Street, Cambridge, from where she had come by the train that day. The lord mayor offered her the choice of a 20s fine or seven days in prison. With no shillings in her pocket, Holloway Prison was the young woman's next destination.

Newspapers devoured the scandalous story. Yet, on the day in question, Daisy had been at home; a policeman confirmed seeing her in Cambridge. Immediately, Lyon suspected foul play. A representative from Lyon & Cade, solicitors, raced to Holloway to uncover the truth.

The young woman, it turned out, had been committed under the name Daisy Hopkins at three o'clock on Wednesday afternoon. By five o'clock, a gentleman had called to pay her fine. He apparently escorted the 'bogus Daisy' back to Cambridge. There was no way of identifying the man; no way of knowing for certain who was behind the trick to discredit the real Daisy Hopkins. But the damage had been done and there was little Lyon could do to remedy the situation.

Finally, on 17 March, the *East Anglian Daily Times* printed a piece of irrefutable truth. The paper announced that on Thursday, 24 March 1892, *Hopkins vs Wallis* would be heard at the Winter Assizes at Ipswich Shire Hall. Mr Murphy QC and Dr Cooper were engaged to represent the plaintiff and Mr Kemp QC and Mr Rawlinson were for the defendant, Wallis.

Immediately, demand for seats in the public gallery of the Shire Hall outstripped those available. The High Sheriff of Suffolk was appointed to issue 'special tickets'. The case had become a cause célèbre. Everyone wanted a glimpse of the infamous young woman who had already triumphed in a court action against Cambridge University. Would she do so again?

By 9.30 a.m. on 24 March, an hour before Judge Mathew was due to arrive, every seat in the gallery of Ipswich Shire Hall had been snapped up. The stakes were high. The London press were well represented. By 10.30 a.m., all were ready, poised with anticipation about what was about to unfold.

However, behind the scenes, one person was wishing they were far away. 'I err ...' Daisy Hopkins stuttered as she and Lyon approached Ipswich Shire Hall. Nerves were beginning to attack her body. 'They'll look,' she whispered as the pair climbed the few short steps into the Shire Hall, where they were ushered towards the larger of the two courtrooms.

'I'll ask the constable to keep your identity a secret till you take the stand,' Lyon suggested. The proposal calmed Daisy's spiralling nerves. It was just as well. She would need all her frail strength for the questioning that lay ahead. Already, Barnwell tittle-tattle had been turned into sworn statements.

For her court appearance, Daisy chose a fetching but sober costume – a jet-black dress with matching three-quarter jacket. Her hat, which did not quite conceal the bushiness of her light brown, almost fair hair, was trimmed with a black feather, and she had added a fine black veil and fur boa to her elegant ensemble.

The constable present stuck to his word. No one knew or cared who the woman in black, sitting patiently in the well of court, just to right of the judge, was until she gathered up her dark skirts to step up into the witness box.

At 10.30 a.m., a court clerk called out, 'All rise!'

Mr Justice Mathew, the 62-year-old Irishman who had the distinction of being one of only three Roman Catholic judges, took his seat. It was hoped that the famous Spinning House case would be called at once. However, no such good fortune was in store. First to be heard was *Jones vs Wyatt*, a 'dry as dust' dispute relating to alleged interference with the right to 'ancient light'. The next case was *Butler vs Leathes*, a sporting slander which was hardly more exciting.

The day endlessly stretched on, but it allowed Daisy to understand how a court worked, in the same way that Emma Kemp had watched and waited over thirty years ago for *Kemp vs Neville* to proceed. Daisy, like Emma, watched as well-dressed spectators drifted in and out, among them Wallis and the vice chancellor.

As the clock passed beyond three o'clock, Daisy fretted her case would not be called that day. She also began to worry, having admired the elegant outfits of the ladies in the gallery, that the black fur boa, complementing her elegant outfit so well, might not be quite the thing for this situation. Somehow, this information must have been communicated to Lyon because, during the afternoon, she replaced the fur with a long, wide white scarf which she draped around her slim shoulders.

It was almost four o'clock when the slander case moved to its conclusion. The courtroom filled in anticipation. Justice Mathew confirmed he would carry on to hear *Hopkins vs Wallis*. He swore in the special jury, whose names the newspapers do not record. The barristers took their seats. They gazed at and shuffled the papers in their hands. This was the moment people up and down the country, and even across the Atlantic Ocean, had been waiting for. Daisy breathed in long and slow as she watched the wigged and gowned men readying themselves for battle – her battle.

Daisy's barrister was first to address the bench. John Murphy QC was a stout and jovial Irishman. Once, when in the company of some younger colleagues, he had maintained he could outrace any of them on the condition he was given a yard start and could choose the racecourse. One of the barristers took up the challenge. The younger man was humiliated as Murphy chose for the race a certain narrow passage in the law courts where his competitor was unable to squeeze past him.

That late Thursday afternoon in March, Murphy began with a powerful, rousing speech. First, he carefully set the scene in Cambridge. In essence, it was a speech that had been heard before, from the inquest into Elizabeth Howe, through to Emma Kemp and Jane Elsden, and now to Daisy Hopkins. The facts had not altered, but the mood of the country had. He joked:

> If it were necessary to protect young men by such exceptional means from certain dangers at a dangerous period of life, then it was equally necessary and important that a woman born in the town of Cambridge should be protected simply because the breath of suspicion had fallen upon her fair frame. These dusty old Charters were drawn up in 1561 with no regard to common sense or common law. In the past punishment had included flogging.

This was true. Murphy had done his homework. The Account Books of the Treasurer of the Spinning House itemise disbursements between 28 September 1748 and 27 September 1749. One of the payments is to Horner Johnson, town crier, for 10s, by order of the vice chancellor, for whipping unruly women – women who protested when dragged inside the Spinning House. The whippings took place on the Market Square. Murphy continued:

> I know an attack will be launched on the character of the plaintiff, and I cannot shut my eyes to the fact that stories of all sorts have been circulated about her. Things have carried so far that a common woman, charged with drunkenness and indecency in London, claimed she was the real Daisy Hopkins.

He referred to the still unsolved mystery of the 'Bogus Daisy' masquerade.

'In some quarters,' he continued, 'every kind of slander and suggestion have been used to cast doubt upon the plaintiff's character.' He went on to attack the Elizabethan charter which 'permitted punishment of those "suspected of evil"'.

In the Vice Chancellor's Court, it is an offence to be suspected of an offence. Evidence given against the girl's character would never be allowed in any court in the kingdom except in this Vice Chancellors Court. At her trial inside the Spinning House, her solicitor wanted to know about the man she was accused of soliciting. He wanted to know the man's name and how she might know he was a university man.

Murphy turned his head to face the jury, and slowing his speech, replayed the crucial scene that had taken place in the Spinning House courtroom last early December. He asked:

Gentlemen of the jury, you might hardly believe this is the year 1892. And why? Because the Vice Chancellor declared knowing the name of the University man was a question that should not be asked, nor would he allow it to be asked. He later reconsidered and the undergraduate, a married man aged about twenty-five or six, with children living in Cambridge, confessed he wasn't wearing cap or gown and that HE had solicited HER.

Cries of 'Hear, hear!' rang through the court as a triumphant Mr Murphy returned to his seat. His speech was the talk of the town for weeks. The fact that Charles Russell had confessed to soliciting Daisy was the point. She had committed no crime under English law, nor, technically, under the Elizabethan charter the university was so desperate to cling to.

Still cherishing her anonymity, Daisy Hopkins felt the ripple of satisfaction surging round the courtroom. Murphy had made fools of Wallis and the vice chancellor.

Next up in the Shire Hall that late afternoon was Dr Cooper. His satisfaction at being in court was only evident to those who knew him, but here was a man determined to finish the work his father had started over thirty-six years ago at the inquest into the death of Elizabeth Howe. He gave a summary of the night of Daisy's arrest, as related to him by Lyon, adding, 'All this for a crime there is no evidence of her committing.'

The name 'Daisy Hopkins' was called. All heads turned as she rose from her seat in the well of the court. With a great deal of poise, she daintily lifted her skirts and reached out a slender, gloved hand to grasp the rail as she ascended into the witness box ready to face the Ipswich jury. There she stood, all eyes piercing through her fragile frame. Whatever she might have felt inside, she knew it was vital she maintained the composure of a wronged woman.

She didn't disappoint herself or Mr Lyon. And she didn't intend to disappoint her mother, who was counting on the glory £1,000 would buy.

Cooper questioned her first, confirming her age, address and place of birth, as they had rehearsed. At first, her voice wasn't large enough to fill the room. 'I was born, according to my certificate, on 14 July 1874.' She paused to give herself a moment to quell her nerves. 'I have lived in Gold Street for about three or four years,' she said with more clarity.

'Do you do any work?' Cooper's voice was gentle.

There was a pause. Her throat sounded dry as she replied, 'No, Sir.'

'Did you at any time do any dressmaking or anything of that kind?'

Another pause before the words could easily pass beyond her tight throat. 'Yes, Sir. I was apprenticed to a dressmaker, but my health failed.'

Moving to the night in question, Cooper wanted the jury to be in no doubt that Daisy Hopkins had not been soliciting in the streets of Cambridge. She was, in fact, he argued, an innocent bystander on the night of her arrest. 'Had you an appointment in Newnham with a young man who was paying his attentions to you?'

'Yes, Sir.' Daisy stuck to the story she'd stitched together as she scoured the dirt from the floor of the courtroom inside the Spinning House.

'Did he keep his appointment?' asked Cooper.

'No, Sir. He was called away on business.'

'At what time did you leave Newnham?'

'Between half past nine and a quarter to ten.'

'Did you go back towards your home in Gold Street?'

'Yes, Sir.'

'Which way did you go home when you left Newnham?' Cooper enquired.

'Past the mill, across Sheep's Green, Sir, then Lensfield Road.'

A map was produced. The jury spent some time tracing the innocent journey Daisy described. But was she innocent? They remained unsure.

The jury listened as she gave the same account of her arrest as Cooper had just described. By then, the late afternoon light was fading fast. It had been a long, tiring and emotional day and Daisy was relieved when Judge Mathew announced an adjournment until the following morning. Dr Cooper, Mr Lyon and Mr Murphy were relieved too. Daisy would need all her strength and composure for the cross-examination that would open the following day's proceedings.

25

HOPKINS VS WALLIS

Confidence radiated from every part of Mr Thomas Richardson Kemp QC. He was a force to be reckoned with. His reputation of showing his victims little mercy went before him. The jury would be left in no doubt about the real reason Daisy Hopkins had been on the streets that fateful December night.

Not far from his industrious fingertips sat a sheaf of witness statements testifying to the 'true' character of the girl who was suing a senior member of Cambridge University. He would prove beyond reasonable doubt that Daisy Hopkins was a young woman the proctors were right to fear.

The character caught in the pages was not the one Daisy was seeking to portray. Nor had it been given on oath. As with the case of Emma Kemp back in 1860, tittle-tattle had been twisted into evidence.

Once more, Daisy picked up her skirts to climb into the witness box of the Shire Hall in Ipswich. Once more, the viewing gallery heaved with onlookers ready to witness how she would perform in the spotlight.

'On the day of your arrest, had you been walking in the street with other women?' Kemp's first question was loaded with insinuation.

'No, Sir,' Daisy replied.

Kemp paused for just long enough to hint that he might know better. 'Had you been walking with a woman named Barker?' He then listed the names of women Daisy had allegedly been seen with. All were believed to be prostitutes. 'Be cautious how you answer,' he cautioned.

Daisy fell silent. She swallowed. Without realising it, her gloved fingers curled round to grip the rail running along the edge of the witness box. For effect, Kemp adjusted the right arm of his gold-rimmed glasses. Still no reply came. He cleared his throat and pressed on. 'Were you seen smoking?'

'No, Sir.' Daisy recovered her voice and determination to win the case.

'Do you ever smoke in the streets?' The accusation that Daisy smoked appeared to confirm that she was a woman of lose morals.

'No, Sir, I do not,' Daisy replied.

Kemp hammered on. His clipped questions beginning to take on a beat. 'I am going to ask you a question about which you must think before you answer. Do you assert that you are a chaste woman?'

Daisy was unsure how to reply. She didn't recognise the word. 'I don't exactly know the meaning ...' she stumbled.

'What?' exclaimed Kemp.

'I don't exactly know the meaning of the word. If you will explain, I can answer.' She was a little flustered now.

'You don't know the meaning of chastity?' scoffed Kemp.

'No, Sir.'

'Do you assert you have never been intimate with a man?'

Her eyes widened. 'Yes, Sir, I do,' came Daisy's clear response.

'Do you swear to that?'

'Yes.'

'Do you know Mrs Bell?' Kemp was back to what he had gleaned from statements about Daisy. 'Does she live in Sun Court?'

'She has lodgings there,' Daisy was clever to reply.

'Have you been in the habit of taking men to Mrs Bell's house and paying her half a crown a time for the use of that house?' He was baiting her. He knew she'd lost her temper inside the Spinning House court, he wanted to prove she was no lady – despite her demure black costume.

She took a breath as she lifted her chin so her eyes met his. 'No,' she almost spat out.

'Do you know a policeman of the name Naylor?'

'I don't.' Daisy was back in control now.

'In the month of June or July, about four o'clock in the afternoon, was the door tied up by some boys when you were inside?'

'It was not.'

'When the policeman came, did he find you and the old farmer behind the door?'

Police Constable Naylor was called. Kemp asked Daisy if she knew him. He thought he saw a flicker of panic cross her face.

'No,' she said. 'But I have seen him in the street.'

Kemp wanted to know if this was the policeman who had found her in Sun Court with a farmer.

'He did not,' she protested. 'He found me standing waiting against the door in Sun Court, waiting for my brother's linen.' The anger in her voice came from the fatigue threatening to wash over her as she fought hard to quell the hot temper rising inside her.

'Have you walked up and down St Andrew's Street with girls who are bad characters?'

'Not to my knowledge.'

Kemp was satisfied with his performance. The jury could be in no doubt about the true character of Daisy Hopkins. He then asked about the household income. Daisy confirmed that Charles Hopkins had found a new job, his wages came to £2 or £3 a week. Her father earnt 15 to 16s a week.

'And how are you paying for this action?'

Mr Lyon was called to answer the question and explained he had been instructed by the plaintiff's family to secure her release. He had employed his London agents. The untaxed costs amounted to £138 11s, of which £98 were out-of-pocket expenses. He confessed he had not been paid any money, except for a sovereign from the plaintiff's brother. There had been an attempt to raise a subscription in Cambridge, but it had utterly failed. He heard that it had reached £25 three weeks ago. Mr Murphy stepped in to shed some light on the promise of funds.

'Did you get a great many promises?' Mr Murphy asked Lyon. It was a question that already hinted at the answer.

'Yes, a great many,' Lyon confessed.

'Do you know why they were not kept?' Murphy was urging Lyon towards the answer he wanted heard in court.

'They were afraid of the university, Sir.' Laughter rang through the court as Lyon confessed the truth.

Next, Murphy called Kirby and Mason, the men who had pinned Daisy against the railings on the night of her arrest. He wanted to counter Kemp's attack on his client by sketching out the arbitrary nature of the evidence against her. He asked the men if they had 'ever seen anything improper take place between her and any man'. Both admitted to never actually seeing her act improperly, 'only in a suspicious way'.

The Reverend Frederic Wallis was next to step into the witness box. He arrived with the assurance of a man defended by a formidable legal mind and protected by the laws of an ancient charter.

'What made you suspicious on the night of the arrest?' Murphy asked him.

'I heard a woman shouting as I walked with my men towards Emmanuel College. The woman was half drunk, but I recognised her to be a prostitute I had arrested before. She said she was shouting to a friend, but it alerted my men to the possibility of "evil" taking place nearby.'

'At the time of the plaintiff's arrest did you suspect her of "evil" and of being a prostitute?'

'Yes, both. I had been warned about her by a woman I'd met on my rounds.'

'This woman,' Murphy enquired. 'Could you tell if she had a grudge against the plaintiff?'

'No,' replied Wallis.

'And probably you did not consider the matter?'

'No, it just served to rouse my suspicions to enquire further.'

'And once suspicion is aroused, it goes on like fire?' Murphy lifted one of his ample eyebrows as if to make the point.

Indeed, he was right. A snide word whispered in the wrong ear sowed seeds of uncertainty about the moral character of a young woman. From then on, she was doomed.

At this point Justice Mathew cut in. 'The issue here is not whether the plaintiff has a bad character. What we need to know is if the proctor had reasonable grounds for arresting the plaintiff.' He was right. The character of Daisy Hopkins prior to the arrest was irrelevant, despite her being judged on it.

Murphy turned to the jury to sum up the case for the plaintiff. It was a long, passionate speech of damnation of the powers of the university. 'This isn't the way to administer justice in an English court. It is an abuse of power,' he said. 'There is no proof of any wrongdoing. Mr Russell is not called. His flight from the country suggests a desire to escape the witness box.'

The man Daisy believed she was engaged to, the man she claimed to have been meeting on the night of her arrest, had also fled Cambridge. Neither man dared rush to her aid when the going got tough.

Murphy continued his damning speech:

Cambridge is a place where a great number of young men with money and hours of idleness upon their hands wander the streets. Yet the University has the power to arrest 'idle' women. If nothing else is to be gained from this enquiry, it has shed light upon the extent to which privilege exists in some parts of the country in the year 1892, and how that privilege is abused.

Applause broke out as he retired to his seat, knowing he had done the best he could for the young woman sitting with a trace of a smile on her pale face as she imagined victory for herself and her family, and vengeance for all the spite she had endured since her arrest.

Attention diverted to Mathew.

I congratulate you, Mr Murphy, on your passionate address. Perhaps if it had been delivered in Parliament it might have had a greater effect than it will in this court. This is not a question between the town of Cambridge and the university, nor is it a political question. The power of the charter legally permits proctors to apprehend women suspected of evil. But this is not an issue for the jury to consider either. What is wanted is for the jury to consider if there were reasonable grounds for suspecting the plaintiff of evil? Had Mr Wallis acted in good faith on information given to him about her character?

He sent the jury off to deliberate.

Few dared to leave their seats as they awaited the return of the jury. Lyon and Cooper shared their concern that Kemp's attack on Daisy's morals might sway the outcome. But no hard evidence of wrongdoing had been detected. According to the law of the land, she was an innocent woman who'd suffered a brutal arrest and imprisonment.

No one needed to wait long for the outcome. It took the dozen men of the jury half an hour to decide the fate of Daisy Hopkins.

In the absolute silence bathing the courtroom, the clerk's voice rang out, 'Are you agreed upon your verdict, gentlemen?'

The foreman of the jury replied, 'We are.'

Justice Mathew lifted his wigged head high as he turned his face towards the foreman. 'Had the defendant reasonable grounds for suspecting the plaintiff of evil when he arrested her?' he asked.

'Yes, my Lord,' the foreman replied.

The collective sound of surprise was heard.

'In that case, this is a verdict for the defendant,' Mathew announced.

Disappointment filled the room. Under the charter, suspicion, even mistaken suspicion, if based on reasonable grounds, was enough to prove a proctor blameless and the plaintiff guilty. Sensing he must qualify the outcome, Mathew signalled he had more to say. 'I must state,' he said, as he threw open and upwards the palms of his hands, 'that all that has been established here is that there were good grounds for suspecting the plaintiff on the evening of her arrest. The proctor acted in good faith according to the advice his men had given him. The verdict,' he wanted to make this quite clear, 'is not a judgement on the character of the plaintiff.'

But it was too late. Lyon and Cooper, not to mention the Hopkins family, were crushed. However, hope for justice came quickly. Newspaper journalists from all over the country were quick to condemn the power and determination of the university to allow such 'low, dirty and unfounded insinuations to be flung at a young woman who, despite her questionable morals', had been treated with intolerable brutality from start to finish. A journalist from *Reynolds Newspaper* in London wrote that he was shocked that women in Cambridge would 'continue to be insulted and slandered in order that all possibility of temptation may be removed from the sons of the wealthy classes'.

A journalist from the *New York Times* – such was the interest in this story – had entertained his readers with daily bulletins of the proceedings in Ipswich, and wrote, 'The verdict caused great surprise among the friends of the girl, who have always believed her life to be blameless. There is no doubt that the case will be appealed.'

But there was no appeal; no compensation money for the Hopkins family; no justice in the minds of Lyon and Cooper. But an editorial in the *London Daily News* thoughtfully predicted that 'Daisy Hopkins must try to find her consolation in the thought that she will one day have her place in the textbooks as the cause, however little, of a great event – the abolition of these antiquated jurisdictions.'

The prediction was correct, the struggle against the tyranny of the university had entered its final chapter and the name of Daisy Hopkins would not be forgotten.

26

THE FINAL CHAPTER - AN ACT OF PARLIAMENT

Daisy's defeat was not the end of the story; nor was the winner's victory worth the battle. The national and international hullabaloo about the powers of the proctors to harass women cast a shadow in the minds of an increasingly liberal government and challenged the generosity of benevolent benefactors. The modern age was hard on the heels of the University of Cambridge.

Fewer people took an interest in Daisy as she traipsed around the streets of Barnwell, now in faded dresses. The cause for freedom she had triggered did not vanish. In the minds of Lyon and Cooper, the campaign to rid the town of the prying proctors and Spinning House was not in tatters. The nation was behind them in condemning the situation in Cambridge, where women could be insulted in the vilest of ways.

Cooper remained determined to claim the prize his father had fought to win. The two men looked at every angle of the situation and realised exactly who they needed to fight the final battle. From the start, John Piele, the vice chancellor, had had his doubts about conducting a trial that muddied together two laws. He knew that for centuries, the arrest of women caused ill feeling in the town. He had to acknowledge that mistakes had been made, women's lives ruined, and with the influx of women arriving at the new women's colleges there was real fear of a ruinous arrest of an innocent young woman. What had been tolerable in a time when the university enjoyed unassailable power and privileges over deferential townspeople had changed. Thanks to the outrage following the arrests of Elizabeth Howe, Emma Kemp and Jane Elsden, the university's authority had gradually been eroded.

In June 1893, with statesmanlike dignity, Piele addressed the Senate. 'A great source of weakness in the powers possessed by the university is that they are now out of accordance with modern sentiment,' he said, making it clear that the past five decades had inflicted unwanted embarrassment and financial injury on the university. He argued that the university could gain from relinquishing powers that had 'ceased to serve a useful purpose'. He reminded the Senate that 'owing to the large number of young women studying at Girton and Newham, the old laws could have unfortunate consequences'. These wise words swayed the last of the dissenters.

On 3 July 1894, Queen Victoria gave her assent to a Bill revoking the 1561 Elizabethan charter that James I had later committed to law. The Bill became the Cambridge University and Corporation Act, instantly terminating the vice chancellor's right to arrest and imprison women who were suspected of prostitution. The new Act also liberated the town and its inhabitants from other ancient restrictions governing trade and entertainment – although it clung to its ability to bestow liquor licenses. It was a glorious moment in the history of town and gown relations – a moment triggered on the damp and misty night in December 1891 when it was decided to 'bring in' Daisy Hopkins.

But before the Bill was parcelled up into a red box ready for the queen to sign, one more young woman was hauled off the streets and into the Spinning House. Ada Elsden, younger sister of Jane Elsden, could only plead guilty to being a common woman after she was found, after dark, in bushes near Christ's Piece with an undergraduate, easily identifiable by his cap and gown. Nor could she, or anyone, rail against the seven-day sentence she received. But it was the last time any young woman would be locked up in the cold and damp cell of the Spinning House.

As the twentieth century dawned, the ugly monument to an ugly feud between the authorities of the town and gown was razed to the ground. It was replaced by a modern police station, a grandly ornamented, Renaissance-style building that was the civic pride of the town. This was a new and confident chapter in the history of the town.

On the morning of Monday, 7 October 1901, the sun shone as the mayor, regaled in ceremonial chains and robes, led a procession accompanied by the chief constable. The parade drew a fanfare of cheers and waves as it left the Town Hall to walk along Petty Cury and into St Andrew's

Street to formally mark the opening of the majestic new building. It was a colourful sight. Behind the mayor came the aldermen in their scarlet robes, followed by the black-coated members of the Watch Committee and the town magistrates and councillors in their robes of office.

Before turning the key to open the oak door nestling between a portico carved with the arms of the borough, the mayor spoke of Thomas Hobson, who had given the land the building stood on in 1628 for the purpose of teaching a trade to the poor. Over the centuries, the place had been used in a disagreeable way, he said, but now the town could celebrate. It was, once again, being used solely for the benefit of the town.

On unlocking the front door, shards of sunlight falling from a large stained-glass window situated at the top of a sweeping stone staircase cast a dappled effect on the mosaic tiles of the entrance hall. The building almost rivalled the ancient colleges hugging the banks of the River Cam. This was a proud day for the townspeople of Cambridge.

Among the swelling, smiling crowd, there to witness this important day, were three women whose lives had been so affected by the building that had once stood on this same spot. Sixty-five-year-old Elizabeth Kemp was now running a lodging house in St Andrew's Street. In 1911, the last discoverable reference of her name suggests her business venture did well. Emma was then living in London, listed as a respectable lady of independent means. The antics of Jane Elsden, who become Jane Funge in 1905, kept the local magistrates busy with her drunk and disorderly life. However, her feisty determination to enjoy life seems to have paid off. She is listed as living to the age of 93, dying in some comfort in Penzance, Cornwall, in 1965.

As for Daisy Hopkins, she would marry Arthur George Kiddy in 1906, have a son in 1927, and die at 36 Gold Street, aged 78. She would never know how her name and fame would touch three centuries.

Sixty years after the passing of the Cambridge University and Corporation Act, the tale of Daisy Hopkins was once again being told in college rooms in Cambridge. In 1954, Peter Tranchell, a lecturer in music, wrote the music, and Harry Porter, a research fellow at Corpus Christi College and keen member of Cambridge Footlights, wrote the libretto, fusing together the stories of Elizabeth, Emma, Jane and Daisy into a one-act operetta, *Daisy Simpkins or The Spinning House: A Concert Entertainment in One Act*.

The 'Chorus of the Light Ladies No. 6' contained some now very familiar themes:

The proctors are intending
To take us by surprise
You know they can arrest us
Upon a mere surmise.

The Bulldogs pursue us out of hand.
They are not subject to the law of the land
But we, for the slightest show of affection,
We get three weeks in the House of Correction.

The Spinning House is grey and old.
The Spinning House is damp and cold.
With a Matron who's been sent,
In order to prevent
Any kindness being expressed,
Any decent food or rest.
The Spinning House is dread and drear.
The Spinning House is our greatest fear.

Although we may be walking
With innocent intent.
Although we may be strolling,
It's never badly meant.
Yet we can be tried, and none defend.
We get imprisoned for twenty days on end;
The Vice Chancellor issues just one direction,
And we get three weeks in the House of Correction.

In fact, there is a Proctor now! Let's go! Come along quickly!'

The operetta was first performed at the May Week Concert in Corpus Christi College on 13 June 1954, three years before Daisy Hopkins died. Further performances were held at Trinity High School, Northampton, on 13 July 1961; Selwyn College Cambridge on 9 June 1962; Christ's College Cambridge on 11 June 1965 – the year Jane Elsden died – and, finally, in Gonville and Caius College Cambridge on 18 June 1989.

Daisy's name popped up again forty years later. In his 'Annual Law Lecture' in 1999, Lord Justice Simon Brown cited the habeas corpus case of Daisy Hopkins – it had created legal history in 1891.

In 2012, Vanessa Heggie wrote an article for *The Guardian* headlined, 'Cambridge University's Victorian Prison for Prostitutes'. She referred to a then forthcoming book by Philip Howell, who argued that the Spinning House was the 'inspiration for those supporting the Contagious Diseases Act'. The article also referenced another article by Janet Oswald on 'The Spinning House Girls: Cambridge University's Distinctive Policing of Prostitution, 1823–1894'.

The Spinning House girls refused to go quietly. Their names won't be found in history books about Cambridge – until now.

SELECT
BIBLIOGRAPHY

Births, deaths and census material can be accessed online at:
www.ancestry.co.uk

Archival Material

Cambridge Borough Coroner: Depositions: Elizabeth Howe,
    4 December 1846.
Cambridge University Library: Spinning House Committal Books 1–3,
    1823–94.
Cambridge University Library: The Case of Daisy Hopkins, 1892.
Cambridgeshire Records Office.

Primary Sources

Cooper, C.H., *Cooper's Annals of Cambridge*, Cambridge Collection –
    various volumes.
Mayhew, H., 'The Cambridge Spinning House Abomination', *Morning
    Chronicle*, 2 January 1851.

Secondary Sources

Black, G. (ed.), *Everyday Ailments and Accidents and Their Treatment at
    Home* (London: Ward, Lock, Bowden & Co., 1892).

Bury, M.E. and Pickles, J.D. (eds), *Romilly's Cambridge Diary 1848–1864* (Cambridge Records Society, 2000).

Leedham-Green, E.A., *Concise History of the University of Cambridge* (Cambridge University Press, 1996).

Parker, R., *Town and Gown – The 700 Years' War in Cambridge* (Cambridge: Patrick Stephens, 1983).

Raverat, G., *Period Piece: A Cambridge Childhood* (London: Faber and Faber, 1952).

Stray, C. (ed.), *An American in Victorian Cambridge: Charles Astor Bristed's 'Five Years in an English University'* (University of Exeter Press, 2008).

Thorold, A.L., *The Life of Henry Labouchere* (New York: Putman, 1913).

Winstanley, D.A., *Early Victorian Cambridge* (Cambridge University Press, 1955).

Winstanley, D.A., *Late Victorian Cambridge* (Cambridge University Press, 1947).

Newspapers

Cambridge Chronicle and Journal
Cambridge Daily News
Cambridge Independent Press
Morning Chronicle
Pall Mall Gazette
The Globe
The New York Times
The Times

Journals

Howell, P., 'A Private Contagious Diseases Act: Prostitution and Public Space in Victorian Cambridge', *Journal of Historical Geography*, 26/3 (2000) pp.376–402.

Oswald, J., 'The Spinning House Girls: Cambridge University's Distinctive Policing of Prostitution, 1823–1894', Open University PhD thesis (2008) in *Urban History*, 39/3 (Cambridge University Press, 2012).

Unpublished Works

Kant, D., 'Daisy Hopkins', MPhil dissertation, Department of
   Criminology, Cambridge University (2008).

Pamphlets

'A Problem-Solving Industry – With the Bookfolders' in *The Deliverer*,
   November 1898 (The Salvation Army Publishing Offices,
   Clerkenwell, London).
Case, Brigadier Winifrede, 'If Ancient Boards Could Speak!', *The Deliverer*,
   April 1930 (The Salvation Army Publishing Offices, Clerkenwell,
   London).
Horsey, S., 'Some Aspects of Women's Life in Cambridge', *Some Stories
   From Victorian Cambridge* (2009).

Printed Reports

'Final Statement', extracted from the Girls Statement Book IV
   (London), p.186a (Salvation Army Archive, London).
'Girls Statement', extracted from the 'Girls Statement Book IV'
   (London), p.186 (Salvation Army Archive, London).

Electronic Sources

Brown, Lord Simon, 'Habeas Corpus: A New Chapter', Administrative
   Law Bar Association Annual Lecture, Tuesday, 23 November 1999,
   adminlaw.org.uk/wp-content/uploads/HABEAS-CORPUS-A-
   NEW-CHAPTER.pdf

Tranchell, Peter, 'Daisy Simpkins or The Spinning House',
   peter-tranchell.uk/site-media/writings/tranchell_daisy_simpkins_
   libretto.pdf

INDEX